D1461639

THE SUBJECT IS WINNING

DALEY THOMPSON
The Subject is Winning

Skip Rozin

Stanley Paul
London Melbourne Sydney Auckland Johannesburg

For Tisha. And for Julie

Stanley Paul & Co. Ltd
An imprint of the Hutchinson Publishing Group
17–21 Conway Street, London W1P 6JD

Hutchinson Group (Australia) Pty Ltd
30–32 Cremorne Street, Richmond South, Victoria 3121
PO Box 151, Broadway, New South Wales 2007

Hutchinson Group (NZ) Ltd
32–34 View Road, PO Box 40–086, Glenfield, Auckland 10

Hutchinson Group (SA) Pty Ltd
PO Box 337, Bergvlei 2012, South Africa

First published 1983
© Skip Rozin 1983

Set in Linotron Baskerville by Input Typesetting Ltd, London

Printed in Great Britain by The Anchor Press Ltd and bound by
Wm Brendon & Son Ltd,
both of Tiptree, Essex

British Library Cataloguing in Publication Data

Rozin, Skip
  Daley Thompson.
  1. Thompson, Daley   2. Decathlon, Biography
  I. Title
  796.4'2'0924   GV1060.7

  ISBN 0 09 151360 5

Contents

Acknowledgements

In any work of non-fiction, the key to telling the story being pursued is access. I would like to express my appreciation to all those who helped me gain access to this story, to Bob Mortimer, to Lawrence Thomas and the staff at the Farney Close School, to Lydia Thompson, to Frank Grigor. And especially to Doreen Rayment, who also housed and fed me during my time in London.

My thanks also to Frank Zarnowski, who opened his extensive decathlon files and never tired of running down obscure bits of information, to Steve Powell and his crew at All-Sport Photographic, and to those other professional observers of athletics who shared their insights with me, either through their work or in conversation. Most notably among these are Kenny Moore and Rob Hughes.

There would be no book if, early on, Clifford May, Bob Christopher and then Anthony Blond had not recognized a good story and then helped it develop. I thank them, and my agents, Dinah Wiener and James Brown, for their faith in that story and in me.

Which brings me to Roddy Bloomfield at Stanley Paul, whose commitment to helping me write my book has never wavered.

Personally, I wish to convey my continued appreciation to the members of my private kitchen cabinet for their contributions of time and individual talents: Joan Acocella, Ann Guilfoyle, Nick Acocella and especially Julie Guibord.

My profound gratitude goes to the athletes whose

story I have attempted to tell in the pages that follow: to Pan Zeniou, Guido Kratschmer, David Baptiste and the others.

And most important of all, I thank Daley Thompson, for his trust.

Skip Rozin
27 February 1983

Photographic acknowledgements

Copyright photographs are used by kind permission of the following: Colorsport, Tony Duffy (All-Sport), George Money, Steve Powell (All-Sport), Skip Rozin, Chris Smith, Ian Welsh.

Foreword

When Skip Rozin first suggested our working together
on a book about winning in sport, the idea appealed to
me. He had come over from New York in 1979, research-
ing an article on the decathlon, and we got along pretty
well. He was a bit odd, always singing old rock 'n' roll
songs, but, for an American, he wasn't at all bad. We
found a lot to talk about and, since so much of my time
is spent driving from one training venue to another, I
reckoned it might be nice to have him around for a few
weeks, if only for the company.

It was nice, but it was also more than I bargained
for. We were together for six weeks. Every day. Every
night. All the time. When I relaxed in front of the television in the evening, he was going through my aunt's
scrapbooks on the couch. While I ate breakfast in the
kitchen, he was making his tea. At Crystal Palace he
would watch me train from under the one overhead
heater that works; at Battersea Park he would station
himself up in the stands in the sunshine, and periodically
check my progress as he made entries in his notebook.
Only at Haringey Sports Centre did I manage any time
off. He will say he was ever alert, but whenever I looked
over to see where he was, I found him stretched out on
the big stack of vault pads, sleeping. Otherwise, he was
always there, watching, taking notes in that little book.
When I went to Bremen for a weekend, he went along.
When I spent five days in Lagos, he went too.

What had been a good laugh for the nine days of his
first visit became a little tense as research on the book

9

stretched on through November 1981 and headed towards Christmas. Maybe it was just too long, and maybe some of the question sessions got too personal. I'm not sure. But I do know that at some point the simple business of getting on with each day stopped being simple and little things became irritating. Things like how loud I played the radio in the car, and how long it took him to finish at a restaurant. Things that would never happen if I were on my own. But that was the point. Usually I am alone. I leave in the morning alone and come home alone. I eat most of my meals alone. I spend between two and three hours a day driving, and that is alone. The focus for all of this is my training. Loud music relaxes me as I drive there and back; eating fast makes the breaks go by more quickly so I can get on with it. My life is totally given to training. All my efforts – consciously and unconsciously, awake and sleeping – are aimed at that. Anything that interferes becomes a problem.

At some point, I became aware how much energy this project was taking up. At that point, I considered calling the whole thing off.

But whenever the temptation got strong, I thought about the possible advantages of what we were doing. I have not always agreed with athletics coverage in England. A lot of sportswriters simply don't do their homework. They concentrate on the wrong things; they ask the wrong questions. To be honest, I don't think they understand athletics, not the field events. This has always been a nation of middle-distance runners – it still is – and so they glorify running. But the rest of athletics, like the discus and the vault, is a mystery to them. A discus throw of seventy metres will be ignored if, at the same meeting, Seb Coe runs the 1000 in 2:13. And the decathlon, well, it just is not part of their world. Most do not know what the ten events are; even fewer can list them in the order they are contested. In a way I understand that. It is easier to get your mind around the running of a mile in under four minutes than to comprehend ten separate events being contested over two days.

So it occurred to me that this book just might be a chance to change some of that. If it were done really well, out of it might come a greater understanding of the decathlon, of what it is and how it is contested, and what it takes to commit your life to it. It is different from being a runner or a tennis player. It is a very special thing, and it takes a special kind of dedication.

And, I guess, there was something else, a little more personal, a little more selfish. I was hoping, ideally, if Skip could do his job well enough, that the book might buy me a little more room to breathe. If people could understand just what is involved in preparing for and competing in the decathlon, it might make this strange relationship between athlete and fan more satisfactory for both of us.

There is a feeling that anyone who performs in public becomes public property. I do not believe that. I do not think it is OK when people interrupt my training, or shove a scrap of paper in my face while I am trying to eat my hamburger between sessions. That might be OK for film stars and pop stars and footballers who are paid by those people, the spectators. But us, we are doing it off our own backs. What I owe them is what I owe myself – to do the very best I can each time I compete, or to stay at home. It means that before I enter a meet I have prepared just as hard as I possibly can and am ready to compete at the top of my form. It means that every time the gun sounds, I am confident of winning. That is as true in an empty stadium as it is before a million spectators. It is the same, because the competition is between me and myself. I know that if I do the best I can, I shall win. And if I do not, no matter what the outcome in the record books, I have failed. It is all very personal.

What I would like is for other people to understand this. Competition is my life – winning is my only goal. Everything I do is directed toward that end and I will

11

never permit anything to jeopardize it. Not personally or publicly. Since winning is the only prize anybody cares about in this world, I would like people to know what it costs. And, also, that at least part of the bill is theirs.

Daley Thompson
1982

1

Haunted

It was late on a Friday afternoon and in the power room of the Crystal Palace National Sports Centre, Daley Thompson was fighting to shake off a dismal mood.

The cloud, dark and heavy, had come on him earlier, while he was working on the shot put. Not strenuous work, just a light refining of his technique. The 1980 Olympic Games in Moscow were less than three weeks away and all he needed to win the gold medal in the decathlon was to maintain the extraordinary level of readiness that he had built up. That was what he was doing, spending a little time with each of the various disciplines, keeping that championship edge without risking injury. He had worked out lightly on the high jump and the pole vault the day before, and the discus and shot put that very afternoon. On other days he would concentrate on the javelin, the hurdles, long jump, and the running distances, the 100 and 400 metres, and on his endurance for the 1500. Every day, of course, he ran in the morning. He always ran. That edge is vital, and elusive.

Then earlier that afternoon, at the Leisure Centre in Crawley, while working on his form with the shot – concentrating on each movement as he nested the 16 pound ball in the crook of his neck, wound his body into a tight crouch, then flew open, heaving the ball up and into the air – a strangeness had descended upon him. At first he dismissed it, forced it from his mind by fixing on his technique: the nesting of the ball, the winding of his body, the flying open. But the mood was relentless and would not be dismissed.

That was unusual. Even at twenty-one, Thompson was accustomed to being in control, not a man who surrendered easily to his emotions. He fought on. He finished his session and carried his two shots across the wet infield of the track, stowing them in the small storage shed, alongside the other balls and discs and spears of his trade. He took an extra moment to think as he changed his shoes, then climbed into his car and began the hour's drive through suburban London to Crystal Palace. Most of that day he had worked alone. What he obviously needed was a little friendly competition.

By the time he reached the sports centre, the place was alive with people. The tennis courts were all in use, a football match was being seriously contested on the near pitch, and kids from all over the London area ran along the walkways towards the huge swimming pools in the main building, the coffee bar a flight of stairs above and the sporting goods store a flight below. Daley Thompson is a familiar figure there, and while he is a celebrity throughout England and in most of Europe, in his own backyard he is a superstar who never fails to draw hearty greetings. The fans are youngsters, usually, from the nearby schools, there to receive instruction at the track or for a visit to the pools. The brash ones follow him with pencil and paper; the shy ones hang back, not wanting to intrude. But even the most timid generate at least a wave, a reaching gesture, a halting effort to touch the local hero. More often than not Thompson responds warmly, but on that day he could barely manage a smile, even for the youngest of the children, always his favourites.

He found half a dozen of his fellow athletes in the power room, working out with weights and exercise machines, and he quickly promoted a session of callisthenics. It was a mad game. There were rapid repetitions of knee-bends, push-ups, sit-ups, running on the spot and squat thrusts, each in sets of ten, then twenty, thirty,

14

forty, back down to thirty, twenty, and ten, followed by forty sets of sit-ups and two or three other kinds of organized physical torture. One by one, the other athletes fell further and further behind as Thompson increased the pace, fleeing some unseen horror. But it was no use; he could not escape.

Turning aside offers of a stop at the cafeteria, he left for the car park, high on the hill behind the stadium. In the time it took to reach the car his frustration had turned to anger. He flung his gear into the boot, got behind the wheel and, with Teddy Pendergrass pouring near full volume from the radio, he drove hurriedly through the rush-hour traffic, westward, across metropolitan London to Worcester Park and the home of his surrogate aunt, his own home since 1979. He found her in the living room, going through three weeks' accumulation of mail. He gave her a quick peck on the cheek, put off talk of dinner till later, and stalked upstairs and into his room, closing the door behind him.

And there he stayed, caught by the mood that had pursued him for hours. He sat on the bed, his feet crossed before him, the look of a troubled man upon his face. There was in his entire body not a bone or muscle less than ready for the test in Moscow. He should win. He would win. Still the cloud hung over him. And it was no stranger. He had come to know it all too well.

Finally he surrendered and let his mind drift back over the past two months, eight weeks of mysterious lethargy, during which he was rarely able to recapture the fighting attitude that had driven him since he was a child. Somehow, somewhere, it had gone out of him. He had no idea why, or what to do about it.

'I'm not sure what worried me, because I never really thought it out,' Thompson recalled later. 'I never really sat down and said to myself, what is the matter, why aren't I doing it? I just muddled through. But for those two months, I couldn't get into training, and I couldn't understand why. I'd just finished my best decathlon ever, and the most important meeting of my life was in

front of me. But I didn't want to go and train. I was fed
up. I didn't have any more push.'

The 'best decathlon ever' had occurred on 17 and 18
May in Götzis, Austria, where he had scored 8622 points
to break Bruce Jenner's four-year-old world record. In
three weeks he would travel to Moscow to challenge for
the decathlon crown that the American had won at the
1976 Games in Montreal and, by winning, establish
himself as the world's greatest athlete. That was the
accomplishment Thompson held above all others,
winning the gold medal. It had served as the focal point
for all his labours, thousands of hours of work over the
last four years. It was the inner voice that woke him
each morning when he was still tired from the workout
of the evening before, that drove him out to the track
when it was cold and wet, that kept him there past the
time he wanted to quit. It had been his reason for living.
But somehow, over those last two months, the voice had
been silenced.

As he sat there, the light slowly fading, pulling him
closer and closer to darkness, he let his eyes roam around
the room. It contained whatever physical things he
possessed. A shelf full of books, most of them sports-
related, the others mysteries. On the wall before him
was the fine stereo he had built over the past couple of
years, and the records and tapes he had collected since
discovering that music had a way of lifting his spirits
when they fell, relaxing him when he felt tense. Over by
the window, neatly arranged along the floor, years and
years of *Athletics Weekly* magazines. On either side, two
huge bookends, were clothes cupboards, occupied almost
exclusively by warm-up and training suits. They also
housed the pride of his wardrobe, 400 pairs of athletic
shoes, one type for every event in the decathlon, others
for training, plus flats for running and plenty of others
just for wearing around, all in an endless variety and
combination of colours. Most were from Adidas, who
supplies all his gear, but there were other brands too,
Nike and Pony and Tiger and others, sent to him from

companies trying to gain the favour of the future champion, wanting their shoes to be photographed on the winner of the gold medal in Moscow.

Winner. That was all he ever wanted to be. Winner in football. Winner at running. And finally, winner of the decathlon. From the very beginning, when he first discovered sport, he knew that was the way. It was as easy and natural for him as knowing liquorice was his favourite sweet. He was packed off by his parents at the age of seven to a boarding school in Bolney, south of London. He found himself there, alone, younger than most of the other students, the only black child, and without any sense of who he was or where he was going. But it was there, over the next nine years, that he was to encounter stimuli that would mould his life. It began with the joy of running. Not scooting around on cracked and cluttered pavements, dodging cars and police and bigger kids, but running straight and free, along open fields, with soft grass underfoot. Then came the discovery of football, and what seemed the boundless exhilaration of pure physical effort became augmented by the thrill of competing and winning. He was only ten when he began playing, and he quickly became very good. He played every day after school, and all weekend long, for three different football clubs. That continued till the art of dribbling and passing and scoring was replaced by a total concentration on speed – explosive speed. He proved to be even better at athletics than he had been at football. Soon he was no longer only a school and club hero, but a budding national star, with his name in the press as the winner of the Amateur Athletic Association junior championships in the 60 metres.

The rest is part of what is fast becoming sports lore. His first decathlon competition, on an obscure track in Wales, alerted everyone in the athletics world with any sense of multi-events; his qualifying for the Olympics at seventeen just a year later confirmed him as a young man to be watched. Subsequent performances – breaking the 8000-point barrier in Madrid in 1977 and winning

17

the 1978 Commonwealth Games in Edmonton – were warnings of the storm that was scheduled to hit during the Olympic year.

But still, prior to 1980 the group of true believers was relatively small. Multi-events watchers form a select family. Decathlon. Heptathlon. Pentathlon. Those are words that may be highly respected on the Continent, but England has traditionally been a nation of runners. Sebastian Coe and Steve Ovett are the athletes today's Briton envisions on a track, charging into the final turn, breaking the tape with arms raised. Most had learned the name Daley Thompson. And they had learned that he wins, but not what he wins. Only a handful had gained any understanding of the decathlon, or any sense of what its test meant. The summer of 1980 was intended to change that. He would break the world record. He would win the gold medal, on television, before an international audience. He and his event would be recognized and accepted. It would finally be settled. Even in England, they would know. Even they would understand.

He had approached that summer with full awareness of its importance and orchestrated his preparation. He began by cutting back on his public exposure, limiting his appearances and the time he would make available to the press. He also watched more carefully what he said to reporters. Confidence in his own ability had come across as arrogance and he decided it was time to let his performances speak for him. He began his physical preparation early in the autumn of 1979, laying down a foundation for the more strenuous work to come. By winter he was putting in three and sometimes four sessions a day, running in the morning, working on skill events such as the shot, discus and vault through the middle of the day, then coming back for weight lifting, callisthenics and often more technique in the evening. He was building, so that by May when the international championships were contested in Götzis, he would be

18

rcady to begin honing his competitive edge for the showdown in Moscow.

'It was never my plan to go for the record in Götzis,'
says Thompson. 'It was too early in the season. You
build, not only in training, but competitively, through
the season, towards a peak. My peak was going to be
Moscow, three months away. That was the perfect stage.
Unfortunately, that wasn't the way it happened.

'I can't even tell you how it did happen. I was in good
shape – mentally and physically – just not at my best.
But I didn't need my best. I didn't even need to be
pushing. There was this momentum that began with the
100 metres, and it carried me through. I wasn't even
trying all that hard, not until the end. The last couple
of events were getting difficult. I was getting physically
tired, and when it came time for the 1500 I was drained.
But I was so close, I had to go for it. I did it, but it
really cost me.'

It was when he returned home from Austria that the
trouble began. 'After Götzis I took my usual week off,
then went back to training. But it wasn't with the same
kind of aggression. I couldn't understand why. I still
can't understand.'

The entire summer dragged on in the same way. He
was plagued by one minor but nagging injury after
another, mostly a thigh that further slowed his training
and forced him to cut back on his normally heavy
schedule of open events, his way of preparing competitively between decathlons. But it was not the injuries
that bothered him most. It was that intangible element
– that hunger – that he missed.

His room was stone quiet, quiet enough for him to
hear himself think. It was a terrible thing to lose that
aggression, as he calls it. It had always helped provide
him with that extra measure of push. He was not the
biggest athlete in the world, not the strongest or the
fastest. But he did have a tremendous amount of energy,
and the ability to channel that energy in a single direction, to marshal every fibre of his being and direct it

towards a goal. It had, since before he could remember, been the hallmark of his personality. Not simply desire. Hunger, savage hunger. It was there when he competed for his local athletics club; it was there when he was at boarding school. It was even there before – at least the essence of it was – when he was growing up in the racially mixed Notting Hill area of London, himself the child of a Nigerian father and a Scottish mother. The difference was, at the time, he had not quite worked out what to do with all the forces so vibrantly generating inside him.

That was a problem. It is not easy to find an accept-able outlet for all that hostile energy, not for a six-year-old boy living in the bowels of a large city. Figures in authority take a dim view of youthful outbursts under any circumstances, and Daley was not growing up in a particularly enlightened, permissive environment. He had more than his share of trouble, especially early. He was, by his own admission, a difficult child. But once he found a medium for his own personal kind of commu-nication and began working it out on the track, the bonding of that aggression with his speed and strength became as his soul. Not so different from a truly religious man and his faith – it was always there, to be counted on, to be used. That was why the summer of 1980 was so unsettling. It was as if, just before he most needed it, his faith had abandoned him.

'It's important that I figure out just what happened,' Thompson said months later. 'When something goes wrong, if I can figure out why, I can correct it next time. But with this I don't know why. It could have been that I was tired. I'd put in a lot of work. Maybe I could manage to keep myself going for four years, and I just couldn't manage four years and three months.

'It could have been the fact . . . I mean everybody has . . . you know . . . a kind of fear of losing.' He paused. 'I don't know, because I never actually thought that.' The words came out awkwardly, as if they were telling of some horrific sin. The instant they were out, they were disowned. Even then, long after the incident, the thought of defeat was treated as the ultimate tragedy, the worst of all possibilities.

Only once had Daley Thompson lost when he was supposed to win. In 1978 he had electrified the athletic world by scoring 8467 points in winning the Commonwealth Games, and headed into the European Championships. While the Commonwealth Games are a proud competition, they are the minor league for the decathlon. The great decathletes come from East and West Germany, from the USSR and the other countries with a tradition in multi-events, and their arena is the European Championships. There Thompson would challenge Alexandr Grebenyuk, the champion from the Soviet Union, and Guido Kratschmer of West Germany, who had come in second behind Jenner in Montreal two years before. Even there, up against such competition and at the age of nineteen, he knew he was the best and would win. But he did not. Somehow, inexplicably, he lost. The experience haunts him still.

'I don't know if I can tell you what it was like,' says Thompson, recalling the disaster in Prague that summer. 'It was a great shock. I didn't think it could happen, but it did. I felt so bad. I couldn't shake that feeling of failure. I was ever so hard to get along with. I walked around the house for days, not answering the phone, not wanting to talk to anyone.

'People tried to console me. They'd tell me they understood, that they knew how I felt. But they didn't. They couldn't. Unless you've been through it, you can't know. It was like I'd died, but nobody's buried me. It was the worst thing that had ever happened to me. I know it shouldn't be that bad, but it was. And there's no way I can make you understand. Nothing is worse. Nothing.'

Not that he actually thought he could not lose. All athletes learn to deal with the reality of defeat. It is as inevitable in sports as growing old: if you compete often enough and long enough, you will eventually lose. The undeniability of that truth is meant to be locked in a corner of the mind, a piece of cold logic, something to balance that pumped-up optimism so essential to the successful athlete. It is kept there, in reserve, so that when defeat comes, it is not an obliterating shock. And Thompson knows that as well as he knows how many times around the track it takes to complete the 1500-metre run.

The problem at Prague in 1978 was not that he was beaten, but that he beat himself. He came there knowing who his opposition was – Kratschmer, the quiet, superbly conditioned athlete from Mainz – and when the West German pulled up lame in the first event and Thompson breezed to victory, he knew the competition had to be over. Of course, all that was over was the 100-metre run, one-tenth of the decathlon. His youth had deceived him into believing otherwise, and when the last event was run, he had lost. He was embarrassed at his own foolishness and shocked that so stupid a mistake could cause so much pain.

Most young men would have accepted it as a lesson well learned. After all, he was nineteen, only on his way to proving himself the best in the world. That is surely the time to learn such lessons, when mistakes can be written off as youth. And on the face of it that is what he did. He learned never to take any victory for granted until it was won. He learned that you can never be certain of winning, but you can guard against surprises by training very hard, preparing your body for anything you ask of it.

But the effect of Prague went deeper than this simple, albeit useful education. There is always that risk with a defeat, especially at the highest level of sport. For when an athlete has competed there long enough, he learns from the overwhelming evidence of his own experience that acceptance, then friendship and love, and eventually wealth, are the rewards of winning. Losing threatens all that. And since Prague was Daley's first exposure to a major, crushing defeat, it was the first time everything he had built up over four long seasons of decathlon competition had been threatened.

No one outside his immediate circle knew how his defeat distressed him. He guarded from the press and even many friends just how much he was suffering inside. Only he knew of the old memories that reached forward in time to whisper, over and over, their pointed message: you must win to survive. You must win, every time.

It was nearly dark, but it was his room and he knew where everything was. He slid to the foot of the bed and, sitting on the edge, flicked on the power of the black Sansui amplifier against the wall. Coloured dots of light flashed in some seemingly secret sequence as he carefully removed a record from its sleeve and placed it on the direct-drive turntable. It was the soundtrack from the Muhammad Ali film, *The Greatest*; he moved the tone arm to the title song. The smooth, deep voice of George Benson began to croon over the large, matched speakers:

> I believe the children are the future:
> Teach them well and let them lead the way.
> Show them all the beauty they possess inside.

As he listened, he could feel the tension ease from inside and he began to relax. Music, it almost always worked. Especially this music.

It was, after all, nothing new by then, this strange feeling. It had been with him all summer, to one degree or another. Some days it slowed his training; others, it sent him home. But the next day he was back on the track, trying to work it through. Whether it was caused by a fear of losing, or by questioning if all the years of work had been worthwhile, or just by being dog tired, it made no difference. He had learned since Prague that whatever got in his way, internally or externally, had to be dealt with, and he had taught himself to take control. He had learned to accept whatever mood came over him, to let it flow around and through him, then go on, turning all his energies, negative and positive, back into the decathlon. Concentrate more, train harder, and win.

23

He had begun this higher education right there in Prague, sitting in the rain on the second day after falling so far behind that he had actually given up – and he fought his way back. Not back far enough to win, but close enough to take the silver medal. Second place. Not good enough, but better than nothing. And he vowed that day never to let himself entertain surrender again, never to let anything block his path to winning. Moscow had been his goal for four years, and he would not permit some temporary malaise to stand in his way. Maybe he did not feel the hunger he had come to count on. It did not matter, not then. The biggest day of his life was only weeks away. The hard training was over; he had done all his work. He needed only to concentrate on winning, and he would win. He could do that, all by himself.

The record came to his favourite part, and he turned up the volume. Benson's voice rose, and the room shook:

> Everybody's searching for a hero.
> People need someone to look up to,
> I never found anyone who fulfilled that need.
> A lonely place to be,
> So I learned to depend on me.
>
> I decided long ago
> Never to walk in anyone's shadow
> If I fail, if I succeed
> At least I lived as I believe
> And no matter what they take from me,
> They can't take away my dignity.

The record ran to the end, and he sat there on the edge of the bed, listening to the needle track along the silent end of the groove. He smiled, and turned off the machine as a knock came at the door. It was his aunt.

'You okay?' she asked, opening the door.

'Never better,' he said. 'What's for dinner?'

2

Patterns

Greatness in sport begins early. Brilliant novelists can take up writing in middle age. The best statesmen frequently come from other professions in their sixties. In many areas, maturity and the perspective of years are prime requisites for getting started.

But true greatness in sport – that state of performing on a plane clearly higher than the competition – always begins in childhood. Though the significance of that beginning may not be perceived at the time, all that is required is a backward look to see how and where it took place. The evidence will be there. Such beginnings have a way of drawing a crowd.

'I can remember going with our mother to his boarding school to watch Daley compete. Even then – maybe he was twelve – he was so superior to everyone else in school. They had a little track, 200 yards around on the grass, and Daley would win. But he wouldn't just win, he would want to win by 50 yards. He would run, and he would run and run. Most people would be content to win and just look around, doing the Ovett bit with the wave, but not Daley. Daley would want to win and win and win.'

The man speaking is Daley Thompson's elder brother, Frank. More than any other single person, he was on hand to document those crucial years when youthful energies were first turned toward athletics. It was Frank who played with him on the crowded streets of Notting Hill Gate, Frank at those early sports days at boarding school, and Frank at many of his first competitions.

Now that the two boys have become men, it is easier to tell they are brothers. A family resemblance has always shown in their faces, but the nine years that separate them made comparisons difficult when their ages were five and fourteen. Now they are easy, with Daley at a fraction under 6 feet 1 inch and approaching 14 stone, and Frank an inch taller and nearly 2 stone heavier, but without the muscular definition of his more athletic brother. Not that Frank did not have his turn at sports when he was younger. But in recent years he has had little time for such recreation. He began working as a boardman and general all-round assistant in a betting shop when he finished school in 1968, and eleven years later went into business for himself. Now he operates two betting shops – one in Southfield and another in Tonbridge – and a fruit shop in Southfield.

'I wasn't bad at sport,' he says. 'I played aggressively. I always did. If I'm going to play I'm like Daley, I like to win. I'm a competitor, but I don't want to win at all costs, which is where Daley is slightly different from me. I consider myself slightly more human in the sense that I don't drop dead if I lose. I've been on the losing side a few times, and I know that's part of the game.

'But not Daley. It's life and death to him. And that's no new attitude. It began long ago. He was a fierce competitor – you could see that as soon as he could walk. He always wanted to dominate a situation. I remember watching him in the street. He was always very competitive with his playmates. Small as he was, if they didn't do what he wanted, they got clumped.'

The streets that made up their neighbourhood – Ladbroke Grove, Chesterton Road, Lonsdale Road, Blenheim Crescent, all places where they lived at one time or another, in ground-floor or sometimes basement flats – were a scene of early racial mixture in London. That mixture was not always peaceful. Repeated sparks of tension between whites and blacks during the early and mid-1950s led to the Notting Hill riots in the summer of 1958. Much of that had eased by the time Daley was growing up; neither he nor his brother recalls colour lines drawn among their friends. 'People don't regard themselves as black or white in Notting Hill,' says Frank. 'You're just from the area.'

There were other distinctions in that neighbourhood besides its racial configuration. It was a typical urban, working-class area, crowded, with few amenities of the middle class. There were no recreation centres, no playgrounds, no parks. Children in search of fun needed to be resourceful.

'Recreation was literally playing games in the street,' recalls Frank of those early years. 'There was no other place. When Daley was really little and our mother would be working and ask me to take him out, I'd take him to a park, but that was Hyde Park, a three-mile walk. I used to push him in the pram. Sometimes we went to Hampstead Heath. We were great travellers in those days. We used to go to Regent's Park, and climb over the fence at the zoo. We were both animal lovers. Still are to this day.

'But playing games was done in the street – the street was an acceptable place to play. All the kids used to play football, no matter how old they were, eight to eighteen. Dodging cars and playing football – on Lonsdale Road mostly, or we used to play down in the mews. There were lots of garages down there, and at certain hours of the day there wouldn't be any traffic. We'd play all sorts of games, like hide and seek, and some silly game with four sticks and a wicket. But mainly it was football. And racing, of course.

'We always used to race. Over the years, I guess we did that more than anything, even later. He was at boarding school and so was I. Different schools. Coming home on holiday, we used to meet at Victoria and take the bus home. We'd race from the bus stop, and I used to carry the case. His case. And we used to race up the road, and he'd get needled if I beat him, which was

27

often in those days. You've got to remember I'm nine years older than him, and I was quite fit.'

He speaks about Daley with the kind of affection you might expect of one brother talking about another. There is pleasure in the memory of a childhood shared. Clearly he is not alone in that. During one particular interview Daley happened to be present, and while most of the time he sat and listened, nodding and smiling, he often interrupted, sometimes rushing to complete stories begun by his elder brother, sometimes correcting the record, sometimes just commenting in passing. There was the story of the two of them playing football and Frank kicking him in the ankles. 'You were a fouler – he was a brute,' injected Daley, laughing. 'I see you remember,' replied Frank. And stories of the Monopoly wars, games admittedly manipulated by Frank, who would buy cheap hotels, then string them together on expensive properties, increasing his chances of winning: 'When Daley thought he was aggrieved, up went the board,' said Frank. 'Even if I played it straight and was winning, up went the board.' 'You never played it straight,' corrected Daley, and they both laughed.

That competitiveness continues today whenever they are together, as they compare everything from degrees of success to their relative strength, each measuring the latter in his own way – Daley, by lifting weights in the power room at Crystal Palace; Frank, lifting sacks of potatoes and turnips. In their friendly byplay is a longing for the regularly shared intimacy that with time has slipped away. For the two men have taken different paths since those days of racing down Lonsdale Road, and the uncompromising commitment that each brings to his pursuits leaves little time free. Frank, with his business interests, his wife and children; Daley, with a training schedule that covers seven days a week, often ten or twelve hours a day from start to finish.

'I think about those days a lot,' said Frank, at one point digressing and turning to his brother. 'Especially going down to Bolney and watching you on sports days.

We'd take a picnic lunch and have good fun. You'd enter everything and you'd win everything. They had to stop that. They made a rule – two events and one relay. They'd never seen anything like you.'

Daley just smiled.

Bolney is in central Sussex, about two-thirds of the way along the road from London to Brighton. Farney Close, the private school Daley Thompson attended from 1965 to 1974, occupies thirty-three rural acres near the village. The school property, seven acres of which are thickly wooded, is home for 112 varieties of trees, an odd assortment of walking, running and flying wildlife, and a one-and-a-half-acre lake containing twenty varieties of fish.

The school was founded by the Reverend and Mrs Percy Wallbridge, to fill a need in their own personal lives. After serving as missionaries in China in the early part of this century, they returned to their home on the Isle of Wight to take up more conventional lives. But after their exotic experiences in the Far East, they found their children had difficulty adjusting to the English schools. They took up the children's education themselves, a responsibility they had begun in China where there was no choice. It did not take long before the children of other families were attracted to their personal style of education and a school was born. Outgrowing their own house, they bought an old estate in Dorset called Farney Close and then, in 1948, moved the school, the staff and the name to Bolney, purchasing a Victorian mansion, where the school has been ever since.

What had begun as a personal venture, in the early sixties became a privately limited company, recognized as outstanding by the Department of Education and Science. It is controlled by a board of governors, on which Percy and Vera Wallbridge, now in their eighties, still sit. Students are recommended by their local education authorities, and the expense of each student is born by the authority, not by the parents.

I first saw Farney Close on a damp, dreary November

morning. Daley said he would drive me to Bolney but would not go in. As we approached the school he began singling out various points of significance on the property. The line of trees that ran along the road, where he used to play, swinging from tree to tree without touching the ground. The great lawn in front of the main building, where he first tested his football skills. There was such enthusiasm in his voice that I thought he was going to change his mind and come in with me. But I was mistaken. He had said he did not want to stop, and he did not.

The school itself makes up its own community, which resembles a tiny English village. The main building, three storeys spread wide across the front lawn, was built onto the estate's original seventeenth-century farmhouse, now part of the east wing. Behind that noble structure narrow streets wind between a series of houses, blocks of classrooms, dormitories, stables and gardens, opening eventually onto a huge area at the back containing the athletic fields.

Even in the cold, thin light of that winter day a friendly feeling of warmth came from that odd collection of buildings, some hundreds of years old and others relatively new, all joining together in a random style that defied regimentation and seemed to symbolize the school's respect for its students' individuality. Even though those students wore uniforms – navy blue blazers, white shirts and striped ties, and grey trousers or skirts – they showed none of the conventional rigidity associated with enforced dress codes.

The headmaster is Peter Lawrence Thomas, forty-six years old, once a successful buyer of ladies knitwear for a large department store. 'It was financially profitable,' he says, 'but I didn't like the business way of winning. I may be kidding myself, but I think I like to win on other people's behalf.' Farney Close is his third position as headmaster. That morning, he talked about the school in his large, sparsely furnished office.

'This is a school which tries, in its own way, to achieve

what the Wallbridges were trying to achieve when they first accepted students other than their own children on the Isle of Wight. That is, to take young people who, for one reason or another, have had difficulty reaching their potential while living at home and attending conventional schools. We have an excellent facility here, with people who care about their work. And with thirty-two professional staff for our seventy-five children, we can give each child the attention he or she needs and deserves.

'It can be a great shock when a child comes here,' said the headmaster. 'Suddenly, at seven or eight years old, being uprooted from his family – that's not easy. Whatever that home situation was, it was his home, the place he felt he belonged. Suddenly he finds himself here. We tell him what clothes he's expected to wear; we tell him the rules he's got to follow. It can be a difficult adjustment. We try to ease them into it. They aren't forced to conform to everything all at once. They learn, but we give them time. We like to think we know how to ease that process along, and we've had good success.'

From a filing cabinet he retrieved an old photograph of Daley going over the high-jump bar. The name written on the back was 'Francis Thompson', Daley's legal name and the one by which he was known at the school. 'I don't know Francis well,' Peter Thomas said, explaining that Daley had left school before he took over as headmaster, 'but my guess is that he would have been a handful at home. You don't learn the determination that makes you a champion – you're born with it. He's always had it, inside.

'I'd like to think we were better suited to deal with that kind of personality than the regular schools, and that we helped him develop in a direction that was beneficial for him.

'Francis means a lot to these children,' he said as he walked me to the door. 'I was here the last time he visited, and you could see it in their faces. We've had

31

graduates who've done well, but not the way he has. He's taken the world by the ears and shaken it, and that's what many of them want to do. And because he's one of them and he's done that, it seems a little more possible for them.'

I spent the rest of the day at the school, talking to some of the people who had known 'Francis' as a student. What emerged was the picture of a bright, animated little boy who, as the headmaster guessed, had been a handful not only at home but there too, a boy who accepted virtually nothing at face value, who challenged everything. And who, upon arriving at Farney Close at the age of seven, had to deal with two difficulties. The first was leaving his family, and the feeling of rejection that normally accompanies so traumatic a change. The second was being confronted with more rules than he had ever seen. There was a specified outfit he had to wear, all kinds of things he could and could not do, and, of course, the routine: up every morning at 7.30, wash, dress, eat breakfast and return to make up the bed; tidy up, clean your teeth and prepare for assembly; classes from nine till one; an hour for lunch, more classes from two till four; homework before dinner, then one hour of free time before bed at 8.30. And no room for negotiation.

As for most new arrivals, the beginning was the hardest, adjusting to all that was new. Beginnings last about a year. That was the autumn of 1965. While Farney Close now has students from most of England's former colonies, then it was almost exclusively white. The fact that Daley was the only black child in school seems not to have added insurmountable difficulty to that first year. Everyone I spoke to remembered that he 'stood up for himself very well indeed'.

From Audrey Cooper, the matron who would have been in charge of the youngest group then, I learned he was 'a normal, active, naughty child, always very popular, always very able. You couldn't help loving him,' she said, 'though you might want to wring his neck now and then, especially when he was having one of his argumentative moods.'

From Peg Kenward, who worked in the kitchen then and still does, I learned that, even as a youngster, he used what charm he had to ease his way along. 'Everybody had a soft spot for him,' she said, 'because if ever he was rude he'd come back and say he was sorry. He'd come back to the kitchen and say, "I'm sorry, Marge." (Everybody else called me Peg, but he called me Marge, you know, trying to get a reaction.) Anyhow, he'd never go out and do his thing and leave you there angry. Never. And if his soft ways didn't work, he had others. He liked his milk. I'd be dealing it out, and he'd get hold of my arm in a vice grip and I'd have to go on pouring it. Playing like, you know, but serious too.'

But the memories of Francis Morgan Thompson that come through most vividly are those from the athletic field. For it was there, starting at about the age of nine, that most of his time was spent. Memories from Cristabel and Frederick Burt, who worked for thirty years for the school, she as the book-keeper and he as groundsman, in Dorset and Bolney. Retired now and living in nearby Haywards Heath, they lived then on the grounds, just off the athletics field, and still remember him out there working on his jumping, long after everyone else had headed in. Memories from Peg Kenward, who thought his future was going to be in football, he was that good. And memories from Matron Audrey Cooper, who admits now she did not always understand what she was seeing.

'Sometimes I used to think he was lazy,' she said. 'Everything was so effortless to him. The other children would be dead on the games pitch, puffing away, and Francis would just go down there, run around, and he was as fresh at the end as he was at the beginning.'

The clearest images of those days come from George Money, who has been teaching English and geography at the school for twenty years. George Money is the photographer who took the picture of Daley soaring over the high-jump bar, and a man in whom Daley found a sympathetic listener. 'He used to come around after classes, just to sit and talk. It was never anything important, or at least I don't remember it that way. Just conversation. He wanted to talk and we did.'

George Money is a strongly built man in his sixties, nicely dressed and with a slow and friendly manner. His photography, just a hobby when Daley was at the school, has in the last seven years been turned into a subject he teaches. As we talked, he looked through the drawers and shelves of his cupboard, moving aside an old box camera and some loose lenses, rolls of film and sheets of negatives, searching for more photographs of the boy only he among the teachers called Daley.

'Everyone knew I had a camera in those days, and many of the children would come round for me to take their pictures. Daley would bring round his girlfriends. But what I remember most is taking pictures on the athletics field, especially when he was jumping. I must have some slides of that around here somewhere. He made it look so easy. In fact he worked darn hard really, although he probably didn't realize it. He had that automatic feel for running. And when he learned to jump it was the same thing. Very good. He used to jump out of the jump pit, as far as I can remember. Yes, very nice. It was very nice to see.'

From the time I first arrived at the school and began talking to members of the staff, present and past, I had the feeling they were holding back information, being protective of Daley's privacy. That was an understandable and commendable attitude. Every once in a while a journalist would make his way down from London, digging around for a story, and it was the staff's rule to divulge nothing. It was not so surprising that they should be reluctant to open up to me, even though I had Daley's blessing. But the longer I was there and the more people I met, the more I began to think they simply had trouble remembering. After all, Daley had left there in 1974, and even then he was one of nearly a hundred students. As the matron confessed when trying to recall some specific details, 'There were so many – it's just so hard to remember.'

That was not the case with George Money. Somehow, even with his inability to recall exactly what happened and when, or specifically what was said on what occasion, so much of the boy and the time remained fresh in his mind. 'You get the feeling, watching these children, they could go on, with luck,' he said. 'We see kids, they've got potential, they've got this, they've got that. But have they got the mental stability to match their physical strength? If they have, there's a chance they'll go on. Daley did.

'Physically, he was obviously gifted. But mentally he had that bit of vital grind, or whatever it is, a mental toughness. He's got resilience. You could see it on the football field, his using his brains. He had something more than the others. He always found a way to fight his way through, even then.

'He took winning very seriously. Oh yes, he wanted to win, and when he won he was happy. He was never vicious, but he never let up. Going, always going. I used to watch him, all the time, running. I can still see him now, late at night, running out there, a shadow moving before the trees.'

Those trees, the fir, yew, maple and elm, grow thickly around the perimeter of the sports area, around the football pitch and the hockey pitch, the running track and jumping pits. Together, they made up the classroom where the young Daley first found himself, then established himself with direction and ability, and then finally excelled. That is a difficult turnaround for anyone, and all the more remarkable when it is accomplished before the age of fifteen. But this is where it happened, nurtured by the school's facilities and by the patience and interest of the people working there. That, of course, and Daley's own personality, till then possibly more of a handicap than an asset. His brother calls that distinguishing characteristic his 'competitiveness'; George Money calls it his 'mental toughness', his 'resilience'. Whatever it is, there, for the first time, it began to work for him.

Daley does not talk often about his years at Farney Close. He does not deny those years, but neither does he speak of them freely. Usually, when he does discuss the school, he concentrates on the softer aspects; what a fun place it was to come to, with its trees and its lake, and the animals that were kept there then, the ducks and the geese, the horses and the cows. Only once in a great while, under some inexplicable conditions, does another reality become partly visible, the way a winter scene from outside comes through a frosted window that has begun to thaw in spots and patches.

'I remember that first day, standing on the platform at Victoria, my little suitcase in my hand. I was saying goodbye to my mum. I remember giving her instructions. "Take care of Tracy [his little sister], take care of the dog, take care of yourself." I was looking forward to an adventure. Then I looked around the platform and saw the other boys waiting for the same train. They were crying and I wondered why. I guess I knew.

'Of course I didn't want to leave home. Nobody does at seven. But I was a pain in the neck when I was little, because I liked doing what I wanted to, and I was always arguing with my mother. So they sent me to boarding school. But it ended up just great. That's the story of my life. I always seem to fall into shit and come up smellin' o' roses.

'My first football match was no golden memory. They don't let you play when you're really young, and I didn't do much of anything for two years. Then one day – it was after lunch – there was this game going on and I got into it. The first time I ever touched the ball I gave away a penalty. The goalkeeper gets the ball, and he's supposed to kick it out. But he couldn't kick it very far, so I told him to give it to me. I picked the ball up, I kicked it, and gave away a penalty. They smashed my head in for that. But I learned. Before long I was playing every day, and three times on weekends.

36

'When I think about it, I backed into track, too. I wasn't so much a troublemaker at school, more an instigator. The headmaster decided it was a good idea if I had more to do. So one summer he took me down to the local club to spend the evenings there. The Haywards Heath Harriers. It turned out all right. I was the best they had, so I stayed.'

There are no statues of Daley Thompson at Farney Close School, no trophy cases celebrating the victories he won on the track or the football pitch. There is nothing concrete to remind anyone of his nine years there.

Even among some of Daley's contemporaries, only a vague image remains, the memory of a brash but lovable kid. That's probably not so different from what has remained of hundreds of boys and girls who have passed through the school since it moved to Bolney. And for some, nothing special was happening during those particular years. One former staff member asked me if Daley was known in other countries, and what they thought of what he did. When I responded that he was known, and that his accomplishments in track and field were respected wherever athletics was respected, the man shook his head, saying that he never would have thought it.

Among others there, such as George Money, the memory is more vivid, more positive. It is of an individual who was making a way for himself. But the strongest picture of Daley Thompson is held in the minds of the students, most of whom were not even there at the same time as Daley. To them, he is something special. The headmaster used the words 'talisman', and 'touchstone'.

One student who I met, a tall, thin young man dressed in football gear, who guided me to the kitchen on his way out for a match, was particularly quiet as he led me through the halls. Then, as he stood by the door and pointed inside to where I would find Peg Kenward, he

37

asked if I worked with Daley Thompson. I was surprised that he knew what I was doing at the school.

'He was here,' he said, as if to assure me that I was in the right place. 'He played football here.' The expression on his face wasn't exactly a smile, but more an affirmation of the validity of his own existence.

Later that afternoon, while I was walking around, inspecting the old mews area that was part of the original farm, I was approached by an attractive young woman in her mid-teens, with short black hair and wearing school uniform. She introduced herself as Denise, and began asking questions as if we were in the middle of a conversation. 'It must be hard to write a book,' she remarked. I responded that it had its difficult moments, trying to conceal my surprise at the efficiency of the school grapevine. 'You're right to, he's worth a book. He's shown them for all of us,' she said. 'That's something.'

3

Lost and Found

Mayesbrook Park is in Barking, far on the east side of
London, a short tube ride from the Upminster terminus
of the District Line. It is not a fancy park, with tennis
courts, bridle paths and a great lake with rowing boats
and swans; not a park where people come on Sunday
afternoons to picnic and listen to concerts. It is more of
a big, empty field, with little grass and few trees, and
lots of hollows that fill up with water when it rains. It
does have a few football pitches, and, at one end, a track
and a set of stands. Behind the stands is a hut for
showering and changing clothes.

This modest setting is the home of the Essex Beagles,
one of London's many amateur athletics clubs. The
Beagles share the track, the field and the shower facilities
with several schools and football clubs, paying £850 a
year to the local council for that privilege. To one side
of the stands is a small breezeblock building, which the
club owns and which serves as their refreshment hut and
clubhouse.

In the summer the park is well attended, drawing
children and footballers every day and on many evenings. But during the winter months, when it seems to
rain every day and the field soaks up the water and
never fully dries out, it is less popular. Then the Beagles
are Mayesbrook Park's most faithful tenants, meeting as
a club on Tuesday and Thursday nights, and on Sunday
mornings, with many of its members coming to train
daily.

It was on one of those Tuesdays in December that I

visited the club. It was about nine o'clock when I arrived, and the clubhouse was crowded with refugees from
the cold outside. Many of the younger members had
been out training, doing their repetitions of 200- and
300-metre sprints, running laps around the badly worn
track. Others were just there to add their support,
huddled in the creaky old stands, watching the goings
on under the dim lights. After all, it was Tuesday night,
and Mayesbrook Park was the place to be for members
and friends of the Beagles. In the clubhouse, two boys
in their mid-teens played a game of darts along the far
wall, a dozen or more people crowded around the bar
on the near wall, and in between children and adults
drank tea or beer or soft drinks at the little tables, or
sat in the chairs lining the long wall that would, if it
had a window, look out onto the field. They drank their
sodas, passed around small bags of crisps, and joked
among themselves, stretching out the social interaction
and warmth before heading home.

Not that it was all that warm inside. Warmer than
outside, where the temperature was near freezing;
warmer than the changing hut, where young boys ling-
ered in hot showers then raced to dry themselves, literally diving into their clothes; but by no means warm.
Few if any had their coats off. But being there is an
integral part of the life of the Beagles. There is an official
social side of the club, too, that usually expresses itself
as some kind of annual dinner, where a hundred or so
of the older members dress up in suits and ties, bring
their wives and meet at a nice restaurant, eat a fine
meal, listen to records of Geoff Love and his orchestra
playing 'Tara's Theme' and 'Intermezzo', and talk
about the good old days, when Jim Peters mounted his
desperate quest for glory. Those are nice evenings, and
important; it is through the financial support of those
senior members that the club survives. But the real social
life of the Beagles is here, in the close little clubhouse,
three times a week, when the young members come to
train and the older members come to watch and coach,

to give time and advice, and anything else that is needed.

I had come by that night, the first of several visits, to meet some of the members, young and old, and to talk with Bob Mortimer. Mortimer holds several positions on the various committees of the Beagles, none more important than coach. By profession he is an accountant for the Royal Borough of Kensington and Chelsea, but in his heart he remains an athlete, a serious basketball player in the London club leagues in the early 1960s, once reaching the semifinals of the national championships, and, before that, as a cross-country and middle-distance runner for the Beagles. His running career was ended by a series of injuries, first a broken leg, and then badly torn Achilles tendons. The injuries, he believes, were the result of overtraining, trying to keep up with the schedule of George Knight, another club member and a world-class runner. Ever since, he has been wary of too much training, a vital and difficult lesson he works to impart to young athletes who are convinced that the harder they train the more they'll win.

Mortimer began unofficial coaching in 1971, working with one particular sprinter who had a motivation problem, and took over the club post a year later. It was in August 1974 that he first met Daley Thompson. 'It was our AAA junior and youth championships at Crystal Palace,' said Mortimer, a nice-looking man in his mid-forties, no longer in running shape but still with an athlete's bearing, and a reassuring way of looking straight into your eyes when he speaks. 'Daley was competing in the youth age group, the under-seventeen group, in the 100 metres and the high jump.'

Even at that point, Thompson had begun making a name for himself on the tracks around London. He had begun simply enough, competing at sports days at school. At fourteen he had run well for the Haywards Heath Harriers, and had come back the next year to win the 200 metres at the Sussex Schools Championships in Brighton and the 200 metres and the high jump at the Brighton

41

and Hove Young Athletes Meeting. He won again at Eastbourne at 200 metres, and placed second in the high jump. But most of that was accomplished on youth and raw power, without the benefit of much coaching, and in regional competition. He met a higher calibre opposition at the English Schools Championships in Shrewsbury that July, and came in fourth in the 200 metres, his worst showing of the season. That was a severe blow to his young ego, but his suffering was far from over.

Though it was mid-August, the day of the Amateur Athletic Association junior championships was cold and rainy. Thompson was determined to redeem himself after his defeat in the English Schools, and this was the perfect setting for such a redemption. The day, however, came and went, and only a few friends and family members in the crowd at Crystal Palace ever knew Daley Thompson was there. His results were not even published in that issue of *Athletics Weekly*.

'I was introduced to him, and told how very good he was,' said Mortimer, who was attending the championships to watch his own boys. 'But by then he had finished, and he looked pretty miserable. I had to drag out of him what he'd done. He made the finals of the 100 metres – I think he came in sixth or seventh – and he didn't do very well in the high jump. I don't think he even made the finals in the 200 metres. He was very disappointed.

'We've heard it often from kids, what they've done. They've done the 10.8s, the 10.9s [seconds in the 100 metres], and they just couldn't do it that day. They get to the AAA championships, the English Schools, things like that, and it just doesn't click. You listen to them, and you don't smile. You encourage them. I encouraged Daley that day. He felt like giving up. I said, "Come over and see if you like us." '

That encounter was pivotal for the young athlete. He had just left Farney Close, and was moving back to his mother in Notting Hill Gate. No longer did he have the school or Haywards Heath to compete for, nor their support when he was in trouble. And he was in trouble that day. He was lost and he didn't know where to turn. He considered giving up – he was that upset by his poor showing. Instead he found a new coach and a new club.

A week later Thompson showed up at Mayesbrook Park. Mortimer put him right in with his best sprinters, and when he showed the ability and potential that had led to his earlier success, it was clear that technique was his problem. As Thompson would admit later, he badly needed a coach. He quickly proved that a little well-directed instruction would not be wasted.

'We had the Young Athletes League final at Haringey on 14 September,' said Mortimer. 'That wasn't even a month away. We tried him out in the 100 metres and the javelin – because the club didn't have a javelin thrower – and he wanted to do the high jump. He did all right in the javelin, he came second in the high jump, and he set a new league record in the 100 metres. We did well in the meet, too. We came third.'

The smile of satisfaction on his face was not only for Daley, but also for his club. Club athletics are a serious business, representing not only recreation and sportsmanship, but pride and the pursuit of winning. That was why, even on such a cold night, forty or fifty young Essex Beagles had come out to the track to train, getting the benefit of instruction from Mortimer and Dave Green and the other coaches there, trying to improve. For many the Beagles are a social activity, a chance to meet other kids, an opportunity for play. Others are drawn by the simple pleasure of working out, learning to be as good as possible, marking improvement on their own scale. But for many others, the appeal of athletics clubs throughout the country is that they provide a different kind of opportunity – the chance to gain a little piece of glory. The chance, at least in one pocket of their lives, to prove they can be winners. Life on the assembly line or behind the counter can be more tolerable if, at weekends, you put on a pair of track shoes and compete to the sound of cheering. Even in December, months before the outdoor track season, they were working, hoping that their next race would bring victory for themselves and their club.

If you are an Essex Beagle, victory is all the sweeter when it comes at the expense of a club like Haringey, which is where Bob Mortimer took Thompson that Saturday for his first club meeting. When it comes to athletics clubs, Haringey is big league. The Haringey Sports Council is a well-organized body, actively financed by its borough. While the council has only been in existence since 1967, what has been accomplished in that time is awesome. Their official handbook unabashedly claims the Haringey Athletics Club to be the 'Champion Youth Club of Great Britain', listing twenty-one pages of affiliated societies promoting everything from angling, archery and football to tug-of-war and weight training. The focal point of all this activity is the New River Sports Centre in Wood Green, where Thompson currently does most of his training. The eight-lane, synthetic surface track is fully floodlit, and there is room for such field events as shot put, discus, pole vault, long jump and javelin. There are also three grass football pitches, one for hockey and one for rugby, all of them floodlit, plus a nine-hole pitch-and-putt golf course. There is a huge, magnificent indoor facility, with space for netball, basketball, tennis, weight lifting, and all kinds of athletic activities, including a 60-metre 'straightaway' for sprints and hurdles. If not the most complete sports facility in England, it is certainly the best in the London area.

Mayesbrook Park, in comparison, is a disaster area. The track is now dirt, down from cinder in its youth. The triple-jump and long-jump courses have been evaluated by athletics experts and judged dangerous. The pole-vault area is sadly in need of repair. The physical space is so limiting that the Beagles' promising young hammer thrower, Paul Head, was forced at sixteen to use an adult-size hammer for his training, because the hammer he was supposed to use – 1.5 kilogrammes lighter – kept ending up in the neighbours' gardens. The only lights are round the grandstands, one set at each end, and look to be an afterthought. They illuminate little more than the area of the track that falls between them and the first half dozen rows of seating. Everything else, including most of the track and the stands, is plunged in darkness.

There are, however, positive aspects of the Beagles' home, beyond the quality of its running surface or the candlepower of its floodlights. Intangibles, such as concern and enormous amounts of affection. The atmosphere in the clubhouse reminded me of the gathering of a large family.

All around, adults were helping children. Two men stood behind the bar, one making tea and the other mixing some kind of red soda concoction. In the corner, another senior member was wrapping the ankle of a young runner, and over against the wall yet another was talking to a jumper about his technique. At one of the little tables a woman helped two girls with their homework while, seated on a chair, one of the club's youngest athletes – just eleven – was being fitted in an Essex Beagles T-shirt, sporting the drawing of two playful puppies on the front. Such activity goes on all the time, not only when the club meets officially, but day and night. Whenever kids want to train, adults are there to watch over them. And unlike Haringey, which has a complete staff of paid employees – a sizeable team including administrators, coaches and maintenance people – everyone at Mayesbrook Park is working for love alone: from Stan Robins, the general administrator, to John Rodda, the club president, and from the coaches to the subscriptions secretary, Brenda Mortimer, Bob Mortimer's wife.

It is almost as if the absence of a top-flight facility has added richness to the experience. Nobody comes to Barking because the setting is luxurious or chic, only because it is theirs. They are all there together, dedicated to athletics in the old British tradition. And, in this club, that is something they come by honestly. The Beagles has been an active harriers' club for nearly a century, and that continues today, despite the recent popularity of sprinting, middle-distance running and the rest of track and field. For a club without a well-equipped indoor facility, those are summer pursuits. But all through the winter months, the Beagles' long-distance runners meet regularly and train at the club's current cross-country headquarters at Chigwell Road in Essex. The club has twenty or so young runners who train there under the direction of Dave Green, and some of the older members still turn up at weekends to run through the country setting. The Beagles also sponsor races throughout the winter season. One typical 'ten miler', held when I was there, listed 396 runners from twenty-four clubs. Prizes included a travel iron, an electric kettle, and £15-worth of meat from S. J. Church & Sons, butchers.

Until this modern era, the best-known Essex Beagles had won their reputations in defeat. Jim Peters, Britain's top marathon runner in the late 1940s and early 1950s, three times world-record holder in that event, was the odds-on favourite to win for England in the Empire Games of 1954. His moment in history came on the same Saturday as the great mile race between Roger Bannister and John Landy, the first time that two men in the same race broke the four-minute barrier, Bannister winning in 3:58.8, Landy finishing five yards behind in 3:59.6. Peters, in the blazing heat of that August afternoon in Vancouver, collapsed just before the finish of the marathon, then tried to drag himself the final 220 yards. He pulled himself to his feet and fell repeatedly, until he finally lost consciousness and was carried away. Four years later another Beagle with international aspirations, George Knight, failed in what the newspapers of the day called 'his vital test' to qualify for the European Games in Stockholm, losing his 6-mile qualifying race.

That frustration in international championships ended in 1978 when Thompson won the Commonwealth

Games for England and the Essex Beagles. By the time he won the Olympics it was hard to find anyone at Mayesbrook Park who could remember when the Beagles were not breaking records and winning titles. Today, on the records chart that proudly adorns the clubhouse bulletin board, Thompson holds fourteen of the club's forty-six records himself, and shares three more as a member of relay teams.

The overwhelming majority of those forty-six records are new, set within the last ten years. Some of that has to do with the fact that records, by their nature, get broken in time. Some has to do with that period falling within Bob Mortimer's tenure as running coach. And much of it has to do with the increased number of black athletes joining what was, not so long ago, an exclusively white segment of British society.

One of the most talented of those young athletes was David Baptiste, who as a fourteen-year-old student in 1973 had won the English Schools 100-metres boys' title. A year later he joined the Beagles, shortly after Thompson. Within a month, in an international competition in Brussels, he set a new British record for fifteen-year-olds by winning the 100 metres in 10.8 seconds against students from Brussels, Paris and Copenhagen.

'Those were really good days,' recalls Baptiste, still an active member of the Beagles. 'Daley and I, working on our sessions, improving our technique, always working, then running around to different meetings. We were still at school – I was fifteen, and I think Daley was sixteen – and we had nothing to think about but our running. It was really good.'

Together with Thompson, Baptiste, strong and compact at 5 feet 9 inches and 11½ stone, made up a dynamic running team for the Beagles. He and Thompson competed against one another in the 100 and 200 metres, and often combined on the same relay team. During their first full season together they piled up victories in half a dozen major meetings, and were the talk of the club circuit.

47

'We wanted to be the best sprinters in the country,' according to Baptiste, 'the two hot boys at the time, wanting to do really well, together. Sprints were a bit of a muchness at that time, and to have two good sprinters in one club was pretty good. It brought the club, and ourselves, a lot of publicity.'

He was talking on another weekday night at Mayesbrook Park, while taking a break in the middle of his session. We were sitting high up in the old stands, having moved away from the chatter of the younger athletes and their fans down at the lower level, and were totally shrouded in darkness. Far below, on the track, twenty or more runners worked on their strides in the weak illumination of the park's two lights. A little more than half of those working out were black, a huge increase from the time Thompson and Baptiste joined the Beagles, seven years before.

'There weren't hardly any blacks at all when I joined the club,' said Baptiste. 'Being in the sprints from the time I was fourteen years old, I realized that most of the kids I raced against, most of the top sprinters, were black. But not in the clubs, not in any of them.

'I didn't think much about it here, but I really noticed it when I started travelling around. It did get nasty a few times, in some races I went to. Some meetings you could tell you weren't at home, in the north, and on the coast. In the north it was plain nobody wanted to speak to you, but in some places it was a real hassle. You had to pull yourself together. No real trouble, not like fights, but you couldn't ignore it, either.

'But then that's one thing good about athletics. When you line up and there's eight of you there, colour doesn't matter. It's how strong you are and how fast you are that counts. There is no class distinction on the track. There can't be, when one man can beat another. That's one thing we were attracted to. We could beat certain people, we could tell them we could beat them, and that was that. Colour didn't come into it.'

It would be naive to assume that whatever racial

prejudice exists in a society as a whole would not exist in virtually every part of that society. Lines are drawn racially in England, and those lines extend onto the field of athletic competition, just as they extend into the factories of British Leyland and the ranks of the armed services. The first time Thompson's athletic exploits earned him mention in the newspaper he was attending Farney Close. He was referred to in print as a 'dusky youngster'. He still remembers that, remembers taking the article to his teacher for an explanation. Even in the Essex Beagles, where a family atmosphere permeates all its activities, there are no black senior members, and few of the black athletes remain after training to drink and socialize in the clubhouse. They are welcome enough, but most prefer to go straight home. So while both Dave Baptiste and Daley Thompson function extremely well in a racially mixed environment – and did when they were teenagers – it was only natural that two young, black sprinters in a predominately white club would find each other.

However the relationship began, what quickly developed was a friendship based on mutual respect, and a shared understanding of the needs each man had as an athlete. Thompson, on Baptiste: 'He was always good fun to be around, always laughing and joking, which is the way I like it. I don't like it being too serious. A lot of coaches don't allow talking in their sessions, and everything has an order to it, "A" goes first, "B" goes second. In our sessions, you could go anywhere you liked, as long as you did your session.

'We were kind of a team. We used to go everywhere together. We used to go to the internationals together; we used to go to the cup championships together, and we used to have good fun. One of us used to get beaten, and it was still in the same vein as when we were training. That's really important.

'Dave had a way of helping you keep things in perspective and of keeping you loose. I remember when we went to Cosford for the junior championships, indoors, 60

49

metres. We were sharing the same room. In the middle of the night, the night before the finals, he wakes me up. "Frank," he says – he always calls me Frank – "I've got to show you this." He turns the lights on, goes to the middle of the floor, gets into a set position, and says, "What do you think of this?" I say, "Great, Dave, great. Let's go back to sleep." Two hours later, I'm fast asleep, he wakes me up. "Frank," he says, "I've got to tell you, I've just had a dream. We're running the 60 final. You got out ahead of me. I stumbled in my blocks. But I still won." That's exactly the way he was. That's how serious he used to take it – not serious at all. It was just another pleasant day out for us. That's how I grew to love the sport so much, because it always seemed that I was having so much fun. And a lot of that was Dave.'

As close as the two athletes were throughout the mid and late seventies, as much as they shared, there was a difference in their abilities on the track. And while that difference in no way affected their relationship, or their feelings towards one another, it did affect their lives.

'I think it was visible even then,' said Baptiste. 'Even at the very beginning – that first year with the club – some of us sensed that something special was happening with Daley. I sensed it. Bob [Mortimer] sensed it. I think Daley's brother Frank sensed he was going somewhere as well.

'And a lot of officials – nameless officials – would come and talk to me, because they knew I was in the same club. They'd take me to one side after a meeting and say things like, "That chap's going well, he's going quickly. I hear he can do this; I hear he can do that." And there was a glow when they talked about him, as if he could do something special. Even the rest of the sprinters, they knew he was going to be big.'

Just what they were seeing is difficult for anyone not intimately connected with athletics to understand. Great performances certainly, there were enough of those. In Thompson's first full season with the Beagles, competing in thirty separate meetings – in as many as three different events on occasions – he came in first twenty-eight times, and second thirteen times, of the fifty-seven times he competed. But there was something more to it, something less absolute than results listed on a board. He exhibited an unusual degree of determination, a single-mindedness, even a willingness to work to the exclusion of everything else.

Dave Baptiste: 'He just trained harder than I did. He trained a lot harder. He had to struggle a lot financially in the early days – I guess I did, too – but he still managed to get the sessions in, whereas I didn't. He was attending college, and had to spend lots of time on the train. Out to Crystal Palace after class, to Mayes-brook Park at night; sessions on Saturday and Sunday. And he got it all in.

'That was the difference in the early days. He got the work in, realizing that he was good, and he was going to be the best. He got it in, no matter what. I didn't.'

When I first met Dave Baptiste, at Crystal Palace in 1979, he was one of the cadre of athletes who were working with Thompson. There was quite a group, friends and unofficial coaches, men who worked with Thompson and took from him as they gave, sharing their energies and their expertise. Pan Zeniou, the decathlete who represented Cyprus in the 1978 Commonwealth Games. Snowy Brooks, another decathlete, who competed for Barbados in the 1972 Olympics. Occasionally Steve Green, who had been an English Schools champion sprinter. When he was home on holiday from San Diego State University, Richard Slaney, the discus thrower. And, of course, Baptiste. They banded together to help each other with their work, and to have another pair of eyes to evaluate their progress. In team sports, there is a natural structure in which this occurs; team mates urge one another on, injecting humour where necessary, and coaches oversee the operation, correcting mistakes, judging technique. But in individual sports, while coaches are often an important part of the process, much of the teaching and the cheer-leading is supplied by the athletes themselves.

Baptiste was one of the earliest members of the Thompson team, and when I first knew him, he was its most energetic. He was the one with the big radio, the bizarre sense of humour, the tireless capacity for one more lap.

'Those were really, really good sessions,' said Baptiste, remembering the time. 'I shake my head when I think about them, they were so intense. I made him work hard. We all did. That's the thing about Daley – you want to help him. He brings that out in you. But it had to change. I couldn't keep it up. He got to the stage, two or three years ago, when he was heading for some-thing big. He was training all day, and I was in the Civil Service, a nine-to-fiver, working for the income tax people. That posed problems obviously. I couldn't get away during the day to train. Maybe if I wanted it more I could have worked it out, but it was tough.'

Baptiste's problem was one that confronts many middle-range athletes. Their sport has a place when they are at school – they train and attend classes. But that ends at about sixteen or seventeen. For those who go on to college or university, it may continue for a while, that final confrontation between sport and the work-a-day world delayed. But eventually those entering the work force must alter their schedules and their lives radically if they intend to continue pursuing athletics as anything more than recreation. Four or five hours of training does not fit easily into a day filled with an eight-hour job.

But by 1979 Thompson had already established himself as a world-class athlete, and therefore eligible for support from the Sports Aid Foundation, a stipend for living expenses and an additional amount for special training needs, money to cover trips to warm-weather locations for training during the winter. Baptiste had not reached that level of excellence and had to fit his training in with his work. He tried to resolve the situation by changing jobs, going to work in a sports shop, but that ended up taking even more time.

'I tried to keep the training going, to see if I could do it,' he said. 'It went badly, to be honest. I couldn't get to meetings, I couldn't get time off to train. I was earning more money, but I was getting beaten when I raced. I should have carried on, even though I was getting beaten, but I didn't. I eased up a while, then I finally laid off. But then I missed it. So I packed in the job. I looked for a job that would leave me time to train,' he said, 'but I decided I'd go on the dole if I had to. That's how it ended up. The money's a bit of a struggle, living on Social Security, but I can make it.

'So I'm back here, training every day at Mayesbrook Park, like when I started. I'm pleased with my progress, and Bob says I'm looking good. I try to get down to Battersea Park on Saturday morning and run with Daley and the boys. That's still good.'

He got up and headed down the ramp toward the track. Four or five sprinters were still out there, getting in the last of their sessions. Baptiste stopped for a moment, and flashed a big smile. 'The Commonwealth Games are the big thing,' he said, 'and, if I can, the European. I'd love to shake up the sprinters.'

4

The Perfect Union

There was a good chance, back in 1975, when the course of his athletic future was being set, that Daley Thompson would not cast his lot with the decathlon. Doing so certainly was not his idea.

But then why should it be? He had recently discovered serious track, two years before, and only since joining the Essex Beagles had he begun to develop his extraordinary but raw talent as a sprinter. With Bob Mortimer working on his technique, he improved dramatically over the winter, and began that 1975 season with great promise. Living back in London, attending Hammersmith College and running with his clubmate, Dave Baptiste, his future as a sprint star seemed secure. He was naturally fast, and he was learning how to be faster. In addition to training with the Essex Beagles, he worked several hours a week with Pete Thompson (no relation), a running coach with the Sussex schools.

But Mortimer, who had quickly become a trusted friend, had a different plan. 'From the time I first saw Daley, I thought of the decathlon,' he says. 'He had such potential. He was tall, and he was big. Actually, early in 1975, he was a bit podgy in the face. "Fat," I remember one coach calling him. But if you're podgy and fast and big, then you can do things like the shot and discus. He's always been big. He's always had that base to do it, and he was always reasonably tall. It was a perfect combination. And for a boy that young, I hated to see him lock himself into one or two events. There's plenty of time for that later.'

Actually, the decathlon had been on Mortimer's mind for some time. While there was an abundance of runners in the country, the decathlon had been an embarrassment. The British junior team had gone to France the season before and been badly beaten. Mortimer felt strongly that this was a situation that need not continue. He believed that he had athletes in the Beagles who could make a better showing than had the national team. But selling the idea to Thompson would not be easy. There was no national tradition for the event – no instant picture flashed to mind at the mention of decathlon. The mile conjured up Roger Bannister; football, George Best or Bobby Charlton. England had never known a champion decathlete. Its only world-class competitor was Peter Gabbett, who scored 7903 points in 1971, when the world record was 8417. Sprinting, on the other hand, while not historically strong in the UK, was highly prized by the black athletic community. Still, Mortimer began discussing the switch with Thompson.

'He wasn't very enthusiastic at first,' recalls Mortimer. 'Daley and I had a lot of arguments about it early on. He was very impressed with his own sprint potential. He thought he could carry on with that. The 100 and 200 – that's what he liked best, and that was what he wanted to do.

'Part of it, at least at the start, was that he had trouble with some of the events. We're talking about things like a 10-metre shot. His discus wasn't very good, either. And he found the pole vault very difficult at first; he didn't really like the event. I wouldn't call what he did vaulting. He scrambled up the pole and threw himself over. But he showed a lot of courage. He's got a tremendous amount of guts, because in the first meeting he ever did in the pole vault he crashed on his back and hurt his bottom. It left no permanent damage – it was bruising and cuts – but he showed a lot of courage in coming back. I remember dropping him off at the station that day and I said, "I'll see you on Tuesday." And he turned up on Tuesday.'

Despite those early problems, Mortimer was confident, especially in view of the national situation. The British junior decathletes of the day were scoring only in the 6000-point range, 1000 points behind their American counterparts and even further behind the young Europeans. By working out on paper what Thompson had already done in the various events, it could be projected that he would be more competitive.

Furthermore, Mortimer liked his attitude. 'There were a lot of good athletes in the club when Daley came over,' he says. 'But there was something about his dedication that you don't normally see in a boy that age. He wasn't so different from them, not really, but he was more easily motivated. On talent and loyalty he was like some of the others, like Dave, and Terry Collins, who was the other top sprinter, but they needed more dragging out than him. He didn't need any motivating. Somehow, they didn't realize how good they could be. Daley did, and he was hungry to get better.

'I was impressed by what he had to do to get to training. Most of those boys lived near the park – that's why most of them joined the Beagles. But Daley lived all the way across London. Two nights a week, right on time, he'd travel out to Barking, and at weekends he'd meet us at Crystal Palace. On weekday nights he would meet me after work in the foyer of the old town hall, or in the High Street Kensington Station, and we would ride out to the park together. Sometimes I would make him get his books out and study, and sometimes we would just talk. You can really get to know somebody on those long train rides. You could see how determined he was.'

After many hours of train-riding and many more of conversation, Thompson was persuaded that the decathlon was worth at least a try, if not a firm commitment. At that point, March 1975, he and three other members of the Beagles – Tim Brooking, Ian Welsh and John Davis – began training with Bruce Longden in Crawley, south of London.

Longden was then Britain's southern decathlon coach. Later he would be named one of seven national athletics coaches, specializing in multi-events. Himself a middle-distance runner and a steeple chaser from the time he was twelve and during his years in college, he began coaching in 1963 at the age of twenty-three. His experience coaching multi-events began two years after that.

'I had been presented with an international athlete, who had already become a decathlete,' says Longden, 'and he educated me as much as anything else. I was fresh out of college, head of department in a secondary school, and coaching hammer and all sorts of things. He taught me what it took to be a decathlete. When Mortimer brought these four guys over, I could see that Daley was a cut above the others. Basically he was a sprinter. But he'd done a little bit of long jump and a little bit of high jump, and he wasn't at all bad. And he had size. The foundation was there.'

According to Longden's thinking, there is a perfect combination of talents that contributes to making a great decathlete. 'You can produce a good thrower, relative to his size and weight,' he says. 'You cannot produce a good sprinter. One must have speed. Daley had speed and he had jumping ability. Those are the keys.'

So to Thompson's already heavy travel schedule was added one more venue – Crawley on Sundays with Bruce Longden. He may not have been sold on the decathlon, but he was giving it a close look.

Meanwhile he continued to concentrate on his running and helped the Beagles amass an impressive streak of victories over the first half of the 1975 season. But slowly, from month to month, new events began to show up next to his name with each *Athletics Weekly* that appeared. Pole vault and shot put along with his high jump at the Southern League meeting at Mayesbrook Park; javelin and shot at another Southern League meeting at Chiswick. He wasn't setting any records, but he wasn't embarrassing himself either. It didn't take long before Longden considered he was ready to be tested.

Had it not been for the injury while vaulting that Bob Mortimer mentioned, Thompson's first decathlon would have been in May in Switzerland, with the rest of the national decathlon team. The fall was bad enough to keep him out of the British League meeting at Brighton, and to cost him the Swiss trip.

So it happened that his first decathlon took place in a small, out-of-the-way stadium in Cwmbran, not far from Cardiff in Wales, on the last weekend in June, less than four months after he had begun his training. Even then, it almost didn't happen. When Thompson and his fellow athletes arrived in Cwmbran for the Welsh Open Decathlon, they were informed that AAA rules prohibited anyone under the age of eighteen competing. Daley at that time was sixteen, a full thirteen months below the minimum age.

The original decision was that he would be ineligible, but after an appeal from Mortimer and Longden, the Welsh AAA agreed to 'bend the rules,' and they permitted their young guest to compete. It seemed an inconsequential gesture. After all, the meeting was 'open' to any decathlete of eighteen years or older. Thompson would be the youngest competitor, hardly a threat to affect the outcome.

Along with Thompson and John Davis, Ian Welsh was one of the Essex Beagles judged by Longden ready to compete in Cwmbran that weekend. He was a high jumper and a long jumper by trade, and had done some hurdling and running. The other events – the vault and throwing events – he was learning along with Thompson.

'If anyone was going to make it out of the original group, Daley was,' recalls Welsh, who was nineteen at the time. 'The other three – myself, Tim and John – were fairly even. One would be slightly better at one thing, the other slightly better at another. Daley was generally above us on 50 per cent of the things, and equal on the rest. But even then, when he went to his first decathlon he surprised everybody. It was out of sight.'

Welsh, who now works as a graphic designer and coaches jumping for the Beagles, remembers the two days as cool and dry, and the facility more than adequate, with an indoor weight-lifting room and good warm-up areas. The three athletes shared a room over the weekend, and generally had a good time.

'The whole works were there,' he says, 'seniors, juniors, all bundled into one and competing together. It was all very informal. Before each event they'd come up and ask what you'd done in the long jump, what you'd done in the hurdles, and then they'd pull you out according to that. There were no strict rules. It was a testing experience for everybody – nobody knew what he was going to do.

'The surprising thing about Daley was his long jump. Believe it or not, his long jump wasn't marvellous. He didn't get any height or anything. He had bags of speed and no height. I believe his best was 6.48. Then that day he did 6.99. Now that was the first two events: he did 11 seconds in the 100 metres and 6.99 in the long jump. From then on everybody watched.

'It was one of those times when you knew you were seeing something exceptional. All the competitors and the officials knew what was happening, and there was this buzz that began after the long jump and never let up. I'll always remember the 1500 metres [the last event of the second day]. It was really late; most of the spectators had gone home. Two or three of the guys said they were going to pace him; older guys, one in the Royal Navy. They'd never met him before, but they were going to sacrifice themselves to get him around in the best time.

'I'd run in the previous race and was utterly knackered. There were about four of us that were flat out on our backs, couldn't move at all, and all the other guys were there, crashed out. Suddenly he was on the track and running, and we were all up, cheering for him. It was a stupendous feeling.'

Thompson's final score was 6685 points, 2000 better than the previous best by a British sixteen-year-old, and within 200 points of the world age-group best. Nobody else among the twenty athletes competing that weekend even came close.

'Years later, when he won the Commonwealth Games, the public suddenly found this decathlete appearing out of nowhere,' says Welsh, who finished eighth with 5175 points and quietly retired from the decathlon. 'But it was obvious to anyone who knew anything about the sport that he was going to get there. Anyone who saw him that day knew that he was going to be the Olympic champion and world-record holder. It just wouldn't be any other way.'

Those in attendence showed their appreciation for what they saw. Though Thompson was classified as 'a guest' and not an official competitor, an agreement between athletes and officials resulted in his getting the winner's medal. Thompson himself was cautious about his performance. 'That first one,' he said later, 'that was an all right kind of one. It didn't seem to be too difficult, but then I had nothing to base it on.

'That was the strange part of it. I had no reference points for what I was doing. All I knew was that I should run 11-something for the 100, do 6.90 for the long jump, 1.95 for the high jump, 50.1 for the quarter. Those were the things I was used to doing. Those were the only points of reference I had. Shot put and things, no idea. Pole vault, you'd have laughed. Two-eighty I did? Maybe 2.80. Boy, I was struggling. Still, after it was over I knew it was something I could do. You have a feeling about those things.'

There was no time off for celebrating after Cwmbran. Thompson went right back to work and within the next ten days he competed in three different meetings, one in West London, one in Kirkby, and one at Haringey.

'He wasn't sold on the decathlon,' says Mortimer. 'He

liked it well enough, and he liked the challenge of it. But he loved running. He saw himself as a sprinter, and he was ever so reluctant to look at himself any other way.'

The complex training schedule continued through the summer. At some point he discontinued his work with the Sussex schools coach, but he went on training with the Beagles three days a week, spent Sundays with Longden, and competed every weekend, running the 100 and 200 metres, in 4 × 100-metre relays, and occasionally entering a few decathlon events, working on his jumping and throwing. The strenuous work showed only positive results. On one particular Saturday midway through August, he broke the Beagles long jump and junior high jump records in a meeting at Ashton playing fields.

Then, on the last two days of the month, he returned to Cwmbran for the AAA junior decathlon championships and scored an astonishing 7008 points, more than the winner of the senior title.

About that time, a lot of people involved with athletics in the UK were getting excited. Thompson, however, remained very cautious. 'He still wanted to be a big sprinter,' recalls Dave Baptiste, who was a party to several prolonged and anguished conversations during that turbulent season. 'It was a big problem – a lot of blood and tears were shed about that. He really, really wanted to be a big sprinter. There was one night we even talked about quitting the Beagles and joining Wolverhampton and Bilston [another athletics club].

'It was hard convincing him that he could only go so far, and then, after that, he wouldn't get any farther. A lot of people saw his potential, especially Bob. He admitted he could be a good sprinter, but said he could be a great decathlete. Still, Daley fought it.'

If that entire year were put into the perspective afforded only by the passage of time, it probably was not until the very end that the conversion was made from one means of athletic expression to another. It just wasn't a simple matter. Thompson could see his path in sprinting; the way was less clear to him in the decathlon. Not only his training but also his life would have to change radically. To make a serious attempt at qualifying for the 1976 Olympics – the trials were in May – he would need to work harder than he had ever worked in his life, every single day, a commitment that meant actually moving in with Bruce Longden.

But toward the end of that season, when he had competed in his third decathlon, a senior meeting with the French in which he set a new British junior record, scoring 7100 points, the decision was made. Even he could no longer ignore the signs.

Daley, reflecting on the summer and autumn of 1975: 'All the time I was training with Bruce, before the first decathlon, I was still thinking of myself as a sprinter. Then, at some time after that, I didn't any more. But I don't remember when that was. It certainly wasn't after the first one.

'I might have been a little resistant to the change. Remember, I wasn't just leaving sprinting – it meant much more. I was leaving something I'd found that was really good for me. And I was leaving friends; I was leaving Dave. It's always difficult to leave your friends, isn't it? It's very difficult. Even now, when I don't see him for a long time, I still worry about the sort of things that he's doing, if he's eating properly. You know how stupid people are.

'There was never a conscious decision to leave sprints for the decathlon. I did one, did another, did a third. Then it was time to do the decathlon. It wasn't that one day I was a sprinter and the next day I was a decathlete. Before I realized it, I was doing it. It just seemed natural, and it's been that way ever since. It's me now, and I can't really remember it being any other way.'

5

The Beauty of the Beast

Jacques Lipchitz was a sculptor in Paris during the first half of this century, a Cubist who helped establish that style of art expressing the geometrical representations of natural forms. Years later, when living in New York, he responded to a young admirer who was having difficulty understanding his sculpture, much of it on a heroic scale, many of its themes taken from mythology and the Bible. 'My art is my medium of communication,' said Lipchitz, then in his late seventies. 'I must speak it well, but you must also know the language to understand what I am saying.'

It is not so different in sports. To understand what an athlete does, to appreciate how he pursues his sport, you must understand that sport. You must speak the language. That is why the decathlon has remained for so long a mystery to so many people. It is one event, but it expresses itself in many languages.

In the world of athletics, the challenge of the decathlon is highly sophisticated. A great sprinter need only run 100 metres in 10 seconds to be world class. A great thrower has only to put the shot 70 feet or throw the discus 200 feet; a high jumper, to clear a bar raised 7½ feet above the ground. While such feats are extremely difficult, they are not complicated.

Which is where the decathlon differs. First, it demands all of these skills and more, though each to a slightly lesser degree. And second, the opponent is not a clock or a tape measure; it is not even the athlete in the next lane. The contest is against the event itself. Over those two days, the decathlon is a great beast, strong and swift, skilled and agile.

Most of all, the beast is cunning. The game is on its ground, and it uses that to advantage. It draws its rival into a simple foot race and when the race is run, it makes long jump the game, then shot put and high jump. Beat it the first time out, and it changes the rules for the second. During the two days in which the battle is waged, the athlete must excel in ten tests of separate skills. All are different; none is like that which preceded it. And only by doing his very best in every test can he hope to win. For in the decathlon, true success is measured by the athlete's ability to be better than he has been before.

Throughout these two gruelling days of competition, the beast never tires. It is as fresh on the second day as it was on the first. And finally, towards the end of the second day, after nine events have been run and the athlete is close to exhaustion, when his muscles are tired and his wind is short and his energy all but sapped, the beast confronts him with the most punishing of tests: he must run with every ounce of strength that he has left for 1500 metres, as fast as he can, pursued by the fear that, if he does not run fast enough, all the labours expended during the preceding two days could be wasted.

And all along the way the beast laughs, for everything that can be considered adversity – fatigue, poor condition of the track, inept officials – works to its advantage. Even when the weather becomes a factor, it sides with the beast. Weather is usually an impartial influence in sport, affecting one side as it does the other; a sloppy field hurts the play of both teams in a football match, slows all runners in a race. But in a wet decathlon, only the athlete is hurt. The 400-metre run is always 400 metres; the shot always weighs 16 pounds. And five years after wind and rain cause a poor decathlon, record books carry only the low scores.

Like any formidable adversary, the beast must first

64

become known before it can be successfully challenged. To know it, you must study it. Every day. Not for weeks or even months, but for years. Contemporary statistics indicate that the average world-class decathlete takes slightly more than four years to reach a level of proficiency where he can score an Olympic-qualifying 7650 points. To be truly competitive on the world scene – scoring in the mid-8000-point range – usually takes six years.

Even with knowledge and work, more is required. Maturity and a deep understanding of the event are essential. The strongest swimmer in the world may be nineteen years old; the most graceful gymnast, fourteen. Strength, skill and talent are enough. But not in the decathlon. The beast is too wily. It demands more. It demands time and study. Bruce Jenner was twenty-six when, in his second Olympics, he won his gold medal. Bill Toomey, also an American, was twenty-nine when he won his. Helge Lovland of Norway, thirty.

What takes all that time is not so much the mastering of the individual tests, but understanding and embracing the total event. The decathlon only *appears* to be ten separate events, loosely strung together to make one super event. That mistake is easy to make. You look at the schedule of a track meeting, and there it is, laid out in black and white. Decathlon. Day One: 100-metre run, long jump, shot put, high jump, 400-metre run. Day Two: 110-metre hurdles, discus, pole vault, javelin, 1500-metre run. Two days – ten events. But that is an illusion, and to embrace it is to court defeat. The decathlon is one event, and understanding that in all its ramifications is the key to success. It must be understood during competition. It must dictate the plan for training. It must permeate every hour of the decathlete's life.

The hidden catch is that the parts don't mesh. They are not ten races of varying lengths, ten throwing events with different objects, or ten of anything else. The beast is a whole with ten parts, commitment to any one portion of which will detract from the rest. If an athlete works too hard on the throwing events, putting on weight and developing his upper body and arms – which is the pattern with men serious about the javelin, shot and discus – he penalizes himself when it comes to the running and jumping events. If he concentrates on running, developing his wind and legs and ignoring his arms and shoulders, he pays the price when it is time for throwing. Clearly, maintaining a proper balance is essential.

None of this is an accident. It is exactly why the decathlon was introduced into the modern Olympics. The ancient Games, which enjoyed sustained glory from the first Olympics in 776 BC until the time of Nero, then staggered on for two centuries before being abolished by the emperor Theodosius in AD 393, had no such event. (Closest was the pentathlon, a military exercise in survival consisting of the long jump, javelin, discus, sprint and wrestling, and represented today by the modern pentathlon, which features pistol shooting, fencing, horsemanship, running and swimming.) The Olympic hiatus lasted until 1896, when the Games were reinstated in Athens, the result of a great swell of enthusiasm for sport across the world and also, coincidentally, of the archaeological discovery of Olympia, the original home of the Games, long buried by earthquakes and floods. But those early Games proved embarrassing to European pride. In the first four modern Olympics, American men won fifty-nine of the seventy-one running, throwing and jumping events. In an attempt to dilute the effect of 'American specialization', the decathlon was introduced in the 1912 Games. Its format – identical to today's event – had been developed a year before in Sweden and Germany, having grown out of generations of multi-event contests, always popular in Europe.

The fact that the plan was foiled in those Stockholm Olympics by an American named Jim Thorpe, an extraordinary athlete of the Sac and Fox Indian tribe who proceeded to win the decathlon and the pentathlon – a five-event competition contested in the Games from

1912 to 1924 – is of secondary importance. The event was born and has been the standard for all-round athletic achievement ever since.

What was never envisioned when the Olympics reappeared is the high degree of dedication that has now come to characterize nearly all world-class athletic effort. During the first half of this century even the most serious of athletes would begin training for the Games only during the Olympic year itself. Few striving for a medal today can afford such an attitude. With rare exceptions, all are athletes who remain in condition from year to year, and it is unlikely that any would try to begin the intensive training for the Games any later than two to three years before the necessary qualifying competition.

Modern training is a Herculean effort that has resulted in performances undreamed of in 1896. In the first of the modern Olympics, the 800-metre run was won in a time of 2 minutes 11 seconds; Sebastian Coe's record for the 800, set in 1981, is 1 minute 41.73 seconds. The discus was won in 1896 with a throw of 95 feet 7½ inches; it took a throw of 218 feet 8 inches in Moscow in 1980 to win. The winning pole vault in 1896 was 10 feet 9¾ inches; the existing record, set midway through 1981, is 19 feet ¾ inch. It is all part of the new world of sport: more athletes, starting younger, growing bigger, working longer and harder, and performing much better.

Nowhere is this pattern more difficult to carry through than in the decathlon. The event simply was not conceived with that kind of sustained determination in mind. It was introduced as a unique test for an all-round athlete. The proposition then was: 'How good an athlete are you?'; not, as is now the case: 'How good can you possibly get?' Even in 1948, when Bob Mathias won his first gold medal, his victory was more a demonstration of his natural ability than a committed quest for excellence. Mathias admits that he had never heard of the decathlon until four months before his first trip to the Games in London, the first after the Second World War. Half the events he had never tried prior to that spring. For his second victory, in the Helsinki Olympics, he trained only during that year of 1952. He was an athlete, of course, playing American football at Stanford University, and he competed in their track programme that season, but that was all.

Today such modest preparation could suffice only at the lowest level, when a young athlete is finding his way, learning those events that are new to him, trying to deal with all ten as a unit. But that is a phase passed through quickly by those who are going to find success. Once the challenge of the decathlon is accepted, a more rigorous schedule is soon instituted. And, for those destined to make a name, early results usually reflect that new commitment. Thompson, in only his second decathlon and only two weeks after turning seventeen, outscored Mathias in his London victory by 183 points (both performances calculated on the 1964 point scale). Just a year later, he surpassed Mathias's Helsinki showing by 174 points.

The world-class decathlete of the eighties has redefined specialization. In an age of narrowing expertise, he is the super all-rounder – the athlete whose speciality is general athletics. Such an accomplishment requires a commitment of energy and training unknown in the decathlon of thirty years ago, and unmatched in athletics today. Training for the forthcoming Olympics begins as soon as the old Games end. Athletes train from six to seven days a week, week in and week out, for four solid years. Conventionally, two or three skills are worked on each day, with running every day and weight training two or three times a week, the schedule stretched out over a two-week cycle. It is the kind of effort which earns decathletes the label 'training freaks' from ungenerous observers. Other athletes manage to build a semblance of conventional living around their sport. Decathletes – especially those at the top – have more difficulty fitting in families, jobs and anything approaching a normal social life during their years of competition. The event is their life.

But it is not only because of the preparation demanded that the beast is such a formidable opponent. Competition is the ultimate crucible in the decathlon. Putting all that knowledge and training together into a good decathlon at a given meeting is one of the toughest feats in sports. Even to complete a successful meeting by international standards requires an intricate integration of efforts over the two days, yet, when necessary, separating those efforts emotionally. The effect of a poor shot put cannot be permitted to carry over and hinder the high jump. But if that shot put had been particularly good, there is a spillover of energy that must be tapped for the next event. And, of course, it must be done again and again and again.

The constant need to reassert excellence provides motivation for one of the most illusive of objectives – the perfect decathlon. To achieve it, the experienced decathlete must accomplish his best score ever – called a 'pb' for personal best – in each event. That may not be so difficult for the young athlete, who improves so quickly at the beginning of his career that pbs are registered virtually at every meeting, but the situation changes radically after four or five years and a dozen or more competitions. At that level, the odds against putting together two perfect days are staggering. It can look so good for so long: the athlete's fastest 100, followed by his farthest long jump and his longest shot. And all the while, the beast is waiting, waiting for one slip off the starting blocks, one wrongly placed foot on a take off, a fraction of a second's loss of control in the air. Yet it remains an ever-present goal, a fantasy plot in the mind of every decathlete.

Daley on perfection: 'The problem with chasing the perfect decathlon is that you always think you can do better, you always think that something went wrong. The best you can do is ten personal bests. That's tough at the top. The closest I've ever seen was Bruce Jenner in 1976, when he did four or five personal bests, four or five really close. But having done that, the next time you

69

go you've got those to beat. It's a good time to pack up, which is what Jenner did. It could be difficult to do it again.'

His message is clear. If you should master the beast for those two flawless days, best take the glory and run. For if you dare return to the arena, there will be some other day in some other meeting when no progress is recorded in the discus or the hurdles or the long jump, and it would win. Again. It always does. Never has it been dominated – by man, technique or invention.

Few athletic activities can claim that distinction. Baseball was for ever changed by the home-run hitting of Babe Ruth. Fibreglass vault poles, super-specialized track shoes, the world-wide running mania – all have made major impacts in sport, but the decathlon has absorbed them all. Because of the complexity of the event, and the complicated, continually revised scoring tables by which times and distances are converted to a point total, it has kept ahead of whatever modern athletics has created to defeat it. By bending in a hundred subtle ways, it remains unconquered.

Since those scoring tables are the means by which achievement is evaluated in the decathlon, it is vital for the athlete who lives and dies by that evaluation to have an intimate knowledge of how they work. Otherwise he has no idea how he is progressing. Out of that need grows an interesting relationship between man and tables. Like a parson and his Bible, they are rarely separated. The tables themselves are published in a small, paperbound book containing dozens of pages of times and distances and their point equivalents. You will find one in the decathlete's bag when he trains, one at the table while he eats, one on his bedside table when he sleeps. It doesn't take long for the most important numbers – the points representing where he is and where he wants next to be – to lodge in his mind. He knows, for example, that running the 400 in 50 seconds earns him 813 points, and that, if by some magic, he could get that time down to 47.8, the points earned would shoot up to 906; and if he could just add 5 feet to his javelin best of 220, he would earn a solid 863 points.

But the tables reveal even more fundamental information than how he might score if everything in a meeting goes the way it does in training. Because of the strange way in which they are constructed, the tables tell an athlete how he can best spend his time in training to earn the highest score. Such careful evaluation is necessary because the current tables, the fifth since the original came out in 1912, contain an imbalance. (Or, more accurately, another – and different – imbalance. The new tables, adopted in 1964, corrected a weakness in the 1950 tables, making it more difficult to rely on one or two events to earn a high score overall, but in doing so they created other problems.) In scoring the running events, improvement at the bottom of the scale is rewarded at a lower rate than at the top. A tenth of a second improvement in the 100-metre run, from 12.4 to 12.3 seconds, earns an additional 19 points; that same improvement from 10.4 to 10.3 brings 27 points. This is as it should be, since improvement is considerably easier at the slower end. But it is the opposite in field events. Five feet of improvement at the lower end of the javelin scale earns more than 5 feet of improvement at the top end. As a result, while an athlete must work on all ten events to remain competitive, he would do well to spend more time on his running if that will result in faster times. This is especially true late in the season, when any measurable improvement is crucial.

There is another inequity in the current tables. The theory behind the number of points awarded for each event is that 1000 points should represent a world-class performance, based on the figures when the tables were last revised. (That revision was researched in 1960 and 1961, approved in 1962 by the International Amateur Athletic Federation and adopted for use during the summer of 1964.) The world record for the pole vault in 1960 was 15 feet 9¼ inches, set by Donald Bragg of the United States. That is an achievement that has since fallen well within many decathletes' reach – Jenner vaulted 15 feet 9 inches in Montreal in 1976, and Thompson cleared 16 feet 1 inch in Götzis in 1980 – making the vault the highest scoring of the ten events. The record for the 1500-metre run in 1960 was set by Herb Elliott of Australia, who covered the distance referred to as the metric mile in 3:35.6. That time has never been approached by any decathlete, which makes the 1500 the lowest-scoring event. Many people involved with the decathlon feel that a fairer set of tables should take points away from the vault and add them to the 1500.

These are among the factors that separate the decathlon from the rest of track and field, the infinite complexities that make it so much more than running 100 metres, heaving a 16 pound ball, jumping vertically over a bar, horizontally over a pit, or even the sum of the ten events. Effort must be generated not only in ten directions, but in such an efficient manner that the athlete works to gain points in those events where progress is best rewarded, while not losing points elsewhere. This is especially true at the top of the performance scale. There, trying to cut each tenth of a second off the clock, to add each centimetre on the tape, is like running into a stone wall. It took Thompson just two decathlons, from his first in June 1975 to his second in August, to reach 7008 points, a respectable figure. It took another two years to reach 8190 points. That was in June 1977, when Jenner held the world record of 8617. To gain the additional points necessary for breaking the record required three years of nonstop work. Now, as he climbs toward 9000 points, the cost of every single point builds daily.

The subtlety of this kind of progress, the intricacy of the scoring, the sophistication of blending the various skills necessary to compete successfully – the very concept of determining success – all make the decathlon an extremely difficult event to understand. It is hard, for example, for fans reared in the tradition of winner-takes-all sports to comprehend an event where athletes can actually be sustained by their own individual progress. While there is always a winner of a meeting, the other athletes are competing at so many different levels – those levels often separated by 500 or 600 points, constituting years of work – that each man views the competition in his own context.

Even watching a decathlon is not easy. Races are run in heats, and top competitors may not be in the same heat, eliminating the head-to-head challenge so exciting in other areas of track. Events like the vault and high jump can take hours, as better athletes pass up early rounds, saving energy, testing themselves only at the greater heights. In major competitions, such as the Olympics, with twenty-five or thirty athletes, the deca-thlon can run for twelve or more hours each of the two days. Even the smaller meetings are long and cumber-some when compared to a neat race. It takes up so much room and time that meet officials separate the decathlon from the rest of the activity, staging it first to get it out of the way, or holding it totally separate, at its own meeting. Crowds, except at the biggest of occasions, tend to be small. Frank Zarnowski, the American economics professor who is the unofficial historian, record keeper, news disseminator and cheer leader for the decathlon in the USA, tells of the Amateur Athletic Union champion-ships in Los Angeles where only twenty-eight people sat in the stands of the Coliseum – seating capacity 73,999 – for the two days of top-flight national competition.

But even for those who make it to a meeting and understand what they are watching, it takes preparation, patience and concentration to appreciate what is happening. Without any of these, the two days can easily pass in a blur of seemingly insignificant numbers. The basic equipment necessary to enjoy a decathlon are a pocket calculator, pad and pencil, a set of scoring tables, a metric conversion table, and a supply of sandwiches. A good announcer is also an important asset, but cannot always be counted on.

The usual confusion at a meet occasionally even affects

the athletes. In Thompson's great performance in Götzis in 1980, he needed a time of 4 minutes 26 seconds or faster in the 1500 to break Jenner's world record. Unfortunately, after the race was run, although he could tell everyone around him was excited, they were expressing their mood in German, not a language in which he is conversant. He couldn't find out what had happened. Had he broken the record? Had he tied it? It was several minutes before he got the news.

Despite what seems like insurmountable odds against popular acceptance, the decathlon remains the symbol of athletic excellence. Though comparatively few people have ever watched a decathlon and fewer have the knowledge of what is required to contest successfully, somehow it is understood that the man who wins the decathlon in the Olympics is the world's greatest athlete. Perhaps that sentiment lingers as an echo of a line supposedly uttered after the first Olympic decathlon. It is written that the King of Sweden, in giving Jim Thorpe his winner's cup, said, 'Mr Thorpe, you are the greatest athlete in the world.' To which Thorpe is reported to have replied, 'Thanks, King.'

Possibly, however, that sense of pre-eminence is the result of some intuitive feeling that even unsophisticated fans have about an athlete who excels in ten events deserving more respect than an athlete who excels in one. Perhaps, they reason, difficult as it may be to do one thing really well, doing ten things well has to be harder. The history of track and field seems to support that contention. It is not so unusual for a world-class decathlete, having failed to reach the very top, to go on and star in one of the single events, but for a medal winner in any open event to then star in the decathlon is almost unheard of.

Somehow, without benefit of research, people seem to sense this. For while great runners, vaulters and throwers break world records and fade into oblivion, winners of the decathlon are one step towards becoming legends. Thorpe, Paavo Yrjola, Mathias, Nikolay Avilov,

Bruce Jenner. These are the names that rise from Olympics past to build the lore of world athletics. In countries where there is an opportunity to turn that fame into financial gain – until recently, primarily the United States – those are the men who have turned up in the movies, on television and on cereal boxes.

The true appreciation for the decathlon, however, comes from athletes, from those who know their own challenge and how difficult it is to meet it, from those who have, at some point in their careers, strayed from the path of specialization into the gruelling world of multi-events, and especially from those who have committed their lives and their energies to do battle against the beast.

Daley Thompson: 'It is, of course, the perfect event. It tests all your skills. It tests running and it tests throwing; it tests jumping and vaulting. It leaves out nothing. Take the 1500. It's bloody endurance. Everything else is speed-based. So the 1500 is the total opposite. That makes the decathlon the all-round test. If we didn't have the 1500 in it, the decathlon would be one-sided. But because it's in, that makes the decathlon what it is.

'Winning is hard to explain. The point is not necessarily to come in first, because your abilities are different. Most important is to do the thing well. If you happen to come first, that's good; but if you do it well and come fiftieth, that's good as well. It's not like a one-off running event, where when you come first you win, and if you come third you're nowhere. Even guys who run personal bests in the 100 and come last are crap. But when guys do personal bests in the decathlon – even by one point – *they're happy*. Then it's been worthwhile. But if they're one point behind their personal bests they've done a useless decathlon.

'That isn't to say that winning isn't important. It is. For some of us, there isn't room for anything else. Especially in the Olympics. For the decathlon, that is *the place*. But the same rule applies: I know if I do my best – if I have a good decathlon – I won't be beaten. And, of course, it's only yourself we're talking about. That's the only person that ever beats you. You try too hard; you don't try hard enough. You haven't practised your long jump run-up enough, your strides are off.

'The beast is yourself. The idea is to be able to control your body, make it do what you want it to do when you want it to do it. That's what it's about.'

6

The Commitment

It is hard for most of us who paddle our way through the mainstream of society to imagine ourselves, at the age of seventeen, making the kind of decision that Daley Thompson made toward the end of 1975. He was a bright, attractive young man, who had done relatively well at school at Farney Close and then at Hammersmith College. He had reached the point when it was time to make some kind of choice about what to do with the rest of his life. His friends began working in a wide variety of fields, from security to computer-programming to aerospace; his own brother chose such a path. Thompson, however, shunned all that. He was, he would later say, casting his lot with the decathlon. Completely and totally, for as long as he possibly could.

Ask him about that decision today and he will tell you that he always knew he was going to be good at something, and that it took him until then to figure out what it was. Once he found the decathlon – and settled in his mind that it was the right choice – there was no need to spend any time on anything else. And as you listen to him, especially with the knowledge of what he has accomplished, that sounds reasonable. But he made that choice in 1975, before Götzis or Edmonton or any of his champion performances, and before anything was proved, selecting an event which at that time could not promise either recognition or maintenance, let alone fame and fortune.

The decision was one for which he sought no counsel outside himself. Many considered it risky. Even the man whose judgement he respected most, Bob Mortimer, his friend and coach, never advised him to bet everything on athletics without having a little something on the side, some trade to fall back on, just in case things didn't work out as he hoped. Though today Mortimer admits it may have been that commitment of time and energy, made so early and so completely, that has helped Thompson get where he is. The absence of that determination, Mortimer acknowledges, surely hurt other talented athletes he had known and coached.

The decision was not popular at home. In fact, it caused an eruption that has never fully healed. Not that the situation in the Thompson household was ever one of continuing stability. Even when Daley was an infant, his parents worked long hours. He entered nursery school at four, and when that ended each day he went into the basement of the same building to playschool until his mother could pick him up when she finished work. Then, when he was away at boarding school, his father died. Daley was twelve at the time. The loss was what you might expect when a boy feels particularly close to his father. To this day he carries his father's picture and he has even journeyed to his father's native Nigeria to help in a fund-raising effort for the national athletics association there.

When Daley left Farney Close in the spring of 1974 and returned to London, he lived in a flat on Lower Wood Court with his mother and younger sister Tracy. His brother Frank was married by then. The flat is in Ladbroke Grove in North Kensington, the neighbourhood where Daley grew up. Changes have taken place there, especially since the race riots of 1958. Today it is a busy, working-class, urban area, with crowded streets lined with shops, and many relatively new multistorey flats. Lydia Thompson and Tracy live in one of those buildings, pleasant and well maintained, overlooking a courtyard cheered by flower gardens.

The three-bedroom flat is comfortable and fully carpeted. It is the fifth of Mrs Thompson's homes, all within a quarter of a mile of one another, all in the same racially mixed neighbourhood.

'This has always been a rough area, but a good place to live,' she said. 'Even before the black people came here, this was a well-known area for thieves and robbers. It's improved a lot in the past few years, with all the better housing.

'All the old places have been taken down, so you can't tell now what it was like. It was a dump. But it was a happy dump. People were good to each other. Black, white, Chinese, anything. It's always been a good place to live, especially if you're a mixed family.

'You've got to remember, we're not actually a black family. We're not a white family. We're a mixed family. I think, being mixed, we're accepted more than if we were completely black. And it's getting more cosmopolitan as the years go by. Take this block. We have Spanish, we have Portuguese, we have them from the Seychelles, the West Indies; we have English, we have Irish, we have Scottish. There are 104 flats here, and we get on extremely well. We always have.'

Born in 1927 in Dundee, Scotland, Mrs Thompson served four-and-a-half years in the Army during the Second World War, packing and preparing equipment for soldiers going overseas. Returning home after the war, she found Dundee quiet, and went south for a London holiday. She has lived there ever since.

A smallish woman with fair skin and light blonde hair, who still has strong traces of Dundee in her speech, she met Daley's father when he was visiting a friend not far from where she lived. He was from the Ibo tribe in Nigeria and had been in England for most of his life, serving in the armed forces and living first in the north and then in London. He was charming, powerfully built, nearly 6 feet 2 inches, and very handsome. He was also industrious, running his own mini-cab company.

'Daley was his double,' said Mrs Thompson, adding that his father called him Daley out of sentiment – and necessity. His own name was Frank, so they called their

infant son Francis. Then there was Franklin, the elder
son, whom everybody called Frank. 'When I called out
for Frank, all three of them turned around. So Daley's
father gave him an African name, Ayodele, which got
shortened to Dele, but it's always been pronounced
Daley.

'That child was a terror from the minute he was born.
He was so hyperactive, you have no idea. He never
cried, but he never slept either. For the first six months,
I don't think either of us ever slept. He was clever at
everything. At nine and ten months he was beginning
to pull up; at fourteen months he was walking, I mean
really walking. He talked at a year, and pretty well, too.
My other children were never as clever as him, not
like that. They were slow, take-your-time children. But
Daley, there was no stopping him. He was on the go all
the time.'

It was, she said, that boundless energy and his fighting
temperament – 'a champion of champions', she called
him, always standing up for his friends – that got him
eventually sent off to boarding school. 'By the time he
was seven he was a handful,' she said. 'He was still
hyperactive. He didn't want to go to bed, he didn't want
to do this, he wanted to do that. I couldn't keep up with
him. And with work, and Tracy to take care of, it was
just too much. And since Frank was in boarding school
and enjoying it – at least I think he enjoyed it – I thought
we'd give it a try. I don't think Daley was very happy
to go to boarding school,' she said, 'not at first. Quite
frankly, it was a killer for me. But at the time, I thought
it was the best thing for him.

'We went down there to view it. He wasn't very keen
on it, but who is at that age? Here he was, a seven-year-
old, his mother sending him away. I can imagine how
the child's mind was working. I tried to explain this was
going to be better for him, but does a seven-year-old
accept that being put away in a boarding school is going
to be good for him?'

She went on talking about the years he was at Farney

Close, about going to Bolney on sports days with Frank and her friend Doreen Rayment, who had been with her at the hospital when Daley was born and seen her through the death of his father.

She talked with great pride about what Daley accomplished while he was at school, about what a difficult adjustment it was and how well he managed. She had no particular understanding of athletics, but she loved watching him compete, and she was especially pleased with his development in other areas, socially and academically. Though being away was hard at the time, she thought the experience was the making of him. By the time he returned to London, he was a man.

'After he'd been home about a year and finished at Hammersmith,' she said, 'I suggested he get a part-time job. He said he was going to be an athlete. He said he couldn't go to school, work and train all at once.'

She sketched in the discussions which followed, angry exchanges that grew in intensity until, given the ultimatum of getting a job or getting out, Daley left. The strain continues to this day. She can, she said, hear it when they speak on the phone.

She started to explain her position, what she had been trying to do when Daley moved out and went to live with his Aunt Doreen, but she stopped. It all happened so long ago, and even then it was an old story: the confrontation between a mother and a son, each with a different view of how he should lead his life.

'There were thousands of athletes like him then,' she said. 'The streets were full of them. I felt what he should be doing was working. I had no idea what his potential was, or where it would lead. I thought I was doing the right thing. If I was wrong, I'm sorry.'

Thompson's commitment to the decathlon is one of those life changes that can only be viewed properly in retrospect. As he has said, he couldn't even tell you when it happened. At the time, it was more a natural progression from what he was doing. Here was this new thing, which was interesting, and he seemed pretty good at it. Always a man for a challenge, he thought it might be fun for a while. Only now, looking back, does his life fall into two categories: the time before the decathlon, and the time that followed.

The difference was a matter of intensity. Until the autumn of 1975, sport was recreation. Even during that summer, when he was living at home with his mother and training once a week with Bruce Longden, his schedule was light, at least by standards to be set later. It was a wonderful game – an extension of play. He worked out four or five times a week, a couple of hours each day, at Mayesbrook Park with the Beagles or at Crystal Palace, or wherever he could find a track. Mostly he worked on his running, with Dave Baptiste or Bob Mortimer or Pete Thompson. Then on Sunday he would meet Bruce Longden, usually at Crystal Palace, and they would work on the decathlon. Or more accurately, Daley would work on being introduced to the decathlon, for at that time they were strangers. Six of the ten events were totally new to him, and the seventh all but new. Never before that spring had he worked with the shot, hurdles, pole vault, discus, javelin or the 1500. The 400 he had run once. And with most of the new events, he experienced difficulty.

'They weren't really a problem,' recalls Thompson, 'because it wasn't serious. It didn't matter then if I did well or badly. It was only that one day a week, and then I went back to running. It just wasn't serious. I was trying it out.'

Then, after the long summer of competing in three decathlons and two dozen open meetings, Thompson made his choice. Suddenly things got very serious. He moved in with Bruce Longden, and enrolled at Crawley College as a full-time student. He studied biology and English literature, but classes were a secondary consideration. Being at Crawley made him eligible for a small grant, which helped him live. It still wasn't easy financially. He relied on friendship, a little charity, and often simply doing without. But he could go on with his training without thinking of anything else, and that was how he wanted it. It was a gamble. Neither his mother nor anyone else knew for sure where his athletics would lead.

'I didn't see it as a gamble,' says Thompson now. 'It was just a way to get to do what I wanted. There was nothing else I wanted besides sport. By going to school I could carry on with that as often as I liked, which was all the time. It was a way – the only way I could see – to continue with my sport for another year or two. I was buying every day, every week that I could, and working as hard with that time as possible.'

Whatever his thinking before that autumn, whatever his reasons, the challenge he was about to take up was different from anything he had ever considered, an undertaking many thought was beyond him. More than once it had been suggested that he was incapable of such a long-term commitment, that, while he was easily excited about a new project, his pattern was to do it well and then move on to something else.

Daley, on the year he lived with Bruce and Sue Longden: 'Thinking back, I can't remember how it all got started. I suppose it must have been his idea – it wouldn't have been mine. We were probably talking about training, and I probably said I'd still got to go to school. He probably said you can come to school down in Crawley, and you can stay with me for a bit. I didn't have a schedule then. I just trained. I used to turn up every day after class and Bruce would tell me what to do. I was new at everything; I had too much to learn to start thinking for myself.

'We started off slowly, working about ten minutes every day, probably four or five days a week. It took a long time to get used to doing it. But then it started to build. Soon we were training every day, Saturdays and Sundays too. And it went really well. I've always been good at assimilating lots of things. We used to talk athletics twenty-five hours a day. I really enjoyed living with Bruce. And I learned a lot, I learned more, living with him for a year, than I could have done training for five.

'We talked about track and field, we talked about the decathlon. We discussed absolutely anything and everything: the history of the event, technique, races that were run and were going to be run. When you've got 365 days you can talk about anything. Everybody's technique. Everybody's form. Everything.

'He had a projector in his house, and we used to watch it all the time. We'd discuss races, then we'd watch a film. It was good. It wasn't on a coaching session basis, but on an athletics basis. We were good together. We sure spent a lot of time.'

Whenever Daley talks about the decathlon, a physical change comes over him. Normally, when answering questions, he remains under control, endeavouring to monitor what he's saying. But when the subject is the decathlon – the event and his involvement with it – his face brightens up and, within a few sentences, he begins to talk more quickly, and with more animation. You can see him reliving physical movements connected with training and competition, and this mental exercise makes him happy. All this was happening as he recalled those months living and working with Bruce Longden.

While there were no decathlons for him to compete in during the winter of 1976, there were plenty of individual events in which to test his new skills, as well as sharpen his old ones, at Cosford and Crystal Palace, and back at Mayesbrook Park. He lost nothing from his sprints and jumps and, though he won no prizes as a pole vaulter or shot putter, he was learning and improving steadily.

During this period, while Thompson was laying the foundation for his future with the decathlon, key changes were occurring in his social life. Until the year before, friendships were mostly a question of who was attending Farney Close when he was. But with his return home, and his friendship with Dave Baptiste, he entered a new era, one that would continue to expand when he began going to Crawley and training with Longden. He would, in a relatively short time, broaden that intimate group of friends on whom he would come to rely in not only the months but the years ahead.

The most conspicuous member of that expanded clan was Richard Slaney, the immense discus thrower. The two actually met during the Sussex Schools championships at Brighton in May 1974, but the friendship did not begin until the school year of 1975–76, when both were attending Crawley College. Slaney was there studying aeronautics. His involvement with sport was inherited from his elder brother, who was a hammer thrower, and began when he was a child. But it was interrupted at the age of eleven when he fell while climbing a fence, injuring his leg to such an extent that special surgery was required to pin the top of the thigh bone in place. For three years he was permitted to attempt nothing even remotely athletic.

'When I got to fourteen and was allowed to do sports again I went overboard and did everything,' says Slaney, who today shows no negative effects of his childhood accident. 'I was playing soccer, rugby, track and field. Trying to make up for all the lost time.'

Though he didn't know it then, his body was about to do some catching up of its own. The injury had apparently retarded his growth during those three years. At fourteen, when they removed the pins from his leg, he was 5 feet 6 inches tall. By the time he was seventeen he was 6 feet 3 inches. He stopped growing for a year, and continued again at eighteen. Today he stands 6 feet 7½ inches tall, and weighs just over 21 stone, close to 300 pounds.

'I used to bump into Daley in the library,' says Slaney, who participated in rugby and track and field for a few years, then concentrated on the discus because he was best at it. 'We began training together at Crawley. When he'd throw the shot and discus, I'd arrange to throw with him. We began working out together in the weight room, then he took me over to Mayesbrook Park and introduced me to Bob, and I joined the Beagles. Soon we were hanging around together. Him being little, I used to look after him.'

The senior member of the group was Clifford Brooks, whose nickname Snowy was given him by his mates in the Royal Navy. ('They're always naming people the opposite of what they are,' says Brooks, a native Londoner of Barbados ancestry.) It was in the Navy that he began his athletics, mostly sprints and jumps, which led in 1971 to training for the decathlon.

A tall, remarkably well-conditioned man, the highlight of his athletic career came early and under unusual circumstances. In the spring of 1972 he requested permission to represent his father's homeland of Barbados in the 1974 Commonwealth Games. An official from that small West Indian island responded, offering to send him to the coming Olympics that very summer in Munich. So Brooks, far from being a world-class decathlete, went to the Games under the Olympic rule permitting each country to send one athlete per event.

He and Thompson met early in 1975, when Daley had just begun spending his Sundays with Bruce Longden. Brooks, then thirty-one, was still working on his decathlon, training more for the joy of it than with any outside goal in mind, but with the same conscientiousness with which he approaches all physical endeavours.

'Compared to what he is now,' says Brooks, who works as a security guard and gives an exercise class at a London health club, 'Daley was a little scrawny kid in the corner. I didn't take much notice of him until after his first decathlon. Then somebody said, "This little sixteen-year-old kid scored 6685 points." That was just under my own score at the time, and I'd been working for five years. The first time I spoke to him, I said something like, "That's a really good score, Daley. I'll have to buck my ideas up." He turned around and said,

"Yep, and next time I'm taking you." Right away I reckoned this kid was OK.'

That initial encounter set the tone for the rest of their friendship. 'Ever since we started training together,' says Brooks, who used to join in the sessions with Thompson and Longden, 'we've always had this competitiveness about whatever we're doing. Whether we're warming up or warming down, or whether we're actually racing, we're competing. It's a good way to train.'

Then there is Panayiotis Zeniou, called Pan, or Zeni. Zeniou was born in Cyprus in 1953, in a small fishing village on the southern coast, not far from Larnaca. His father came to England in 1962 and, after getting settled, brought Zeni, his brother, three sisters and their mother to London to live.

Zeniou looks Greek. People meeting him for the first time know he's from Greece before he says a word – which would clear up any doubt. He is an attractive man of medium height and weight, with brown curly hair, a thick moustache, and lots of dark body hair.

He began in sport as a schoolboy in England, showing talent in football, basketball and cricket yet excelling in none of them. But when he picked up a javelin for the first time and then discovered track and field, he felt himself moving to another level. Here was something he could do really well.

At seventeen he joined the North London Athletics Club, where he was introduced to multi-events. The coach there recognized his all-round ability, and suggested he try his first pentathlon. He did, found it to his liking, and in 1972 entered his first decathlon, winning that Middlesex competition with a score, as he recalls, 'of around 5300 points'.

'I met Daley in 1975 at Haringey,' says Zeniou. 'A friend of mine told me the previous day that this kid had won the Welsh decathlon with a score of just over 6600 points, and I said I didn't believe it. Nobody can do 6600 at that age. He pointed him out to me that day. I didn't say anything, other than hello. But I was impressed. Then we met later. We did the AAA. He won the junior and I won the senior in 1975, and then we did the international together. We've been friends ever since.'

Zeniou, who works as a recreation supervisor in north London so that he can devote large portions of time to training, remembers what it was like to encounter such a talented young athlete at a time when he himself was fighting for international recognition in the decathlon. 'His score at the AAA was just over 7000, and mine was just under 7000. He overshadowed everything around him. He showed you how inadequate an athlete you were. And that was then. He was just starting. You knew it wouldn't be long before he was doing that to the whole world.'

Slaney, the dependable giant. Brooks, the voice of maturity. Zeniou, chief cheer leader and keeper of the faith. They were the three new friends found within months of one another during the winter of 1975, Thompson's second season in London after nine years at Farney Close. They joined Dave Baptiste to make up a trusted inner core of people on whom Thompson relies to this day.

The glue of Daley's support system is Doreen Rayment, his Auntie Doreen. It seems that she was always there when he got into a tight spot, when he was a child, when he was at school, and after his return to London. During that first winter he attended Crawley College, he would turn up on her doorstep whenever he felt he had nowhere to go at weekends.

Doreen Rayment is a plucky little lady in her late forties, with curly hair and a quick wit. She and Daley's mother had been close friends for a long time, which accounts for her being at the hospital on the occasion of the birth of Lydia Thompson's second son. 'He looked like any newborn baby,' says Mrs Rayment of that first meeting, 'like a squeezed-up orange, red and ugly. But even then, he was lovable.'

That was the beginning of a long and intimate

relationship. 'It was only natural that we should be close,' she says. 'His mother was my best friend, and we were together every day. I used to spend lots of time at the house, sleep there at weekends, and was generally around him all the time. Later, after he went to boarding school, I used to drive his mother down to see him on visiting days, and he'd visit me whenever he came home on holiday.'

Mrs Rayment, affectionately referred to as Auntie Dodo, has for the last few years held the position of administrator at the Kensington and Chelsea Play Association, a youth recreation programme serving the borough. Her work gave her an understanding and appreciation of athletics and, when Daley was home from boarding school during the summer, she helped channel him into those programmes best suited to his talents and interests.

Then, when Thompson became more serious about his athletics and began entering competitions around London, it was she who frequently provided the transport, moral support and, when necessary, the money for a new track suit or pair of running shoes.

It was Doreen Rayment who engineered the meeting between Thompson and Bob Mortimer. In his position as accountant for the Borough of Kensington, he had regular contact with her in her work with the recreation programme. Knowing of his involvement with the Essex Beagles, she mentioned Daley on many occasions, keeping him abreast of the boy's accomplishments on the track. And, on that rainy August afternoon at Crystal Palace, when Daley was competing on his own after returning from Farney Close, and Mortimer was there with the Beagles, she introduced them.

Within weeks Daley was an Essex Beagle, but that was not the end of Mrs Rayment's involvement with his athletic career. There was, she explains, more of a need. 'In this country there are a tremendous number of young, talented black kids of twelve, thirteen, fourteen and fifteen in sport. Daley started off just like one of those, along with kids like Dave Baptiste and others I can think of.

'The difficulty that arises is that there is no back-up system to help them over the humps. There's so much effort to get them involved with sport and teach them at a young age. But what happens after they're brought along? When they leave school, there is no help until they reach the senior level, unless of course they happen to have a family who will help them and support them, that will take them to meetings and buy their spikes.

'I'm talking about financial help – money. There's nothing at the grassroots to help them, and that's why a lot of talent goes through the nets. I was determined that wasn't going to happen to Daley. I see it a lot in my job. I see loads of kids with lots of potential, and once they leave school they have to fight the wars and get a job and make a living, and they have to let their sport go.

'In many cases it's tragic. I don't mean all those kids who belong to clubs just for recreation, because staying in shape feels good and competing is fun. I'm talking about the others, those who are more serious, those with a dream. It's quite an expense to have a kid who's really into athletics, who comes in and says, "I'm competing in Liverpool on Saturday." Well, that's 300 miles away. What are you supposed to do?'

What she did was to pile Daley and as many of his mates as would fit into her car and drive to Liverpool, or Shrewsbury or Cwmbran or wherever the meeting happened to be. She made his athletics – as well as himself – part of her life. So it was only natural that, when Daley and his mother reached a standoff position about him and his future in athletics, it should be his Aunt Doreen to whom he turned. There was no one else. Though her two-room flat in Maida Vale was hardly big enough for herself and her own son, it quickly became expanded to fit one more.

When, during that winter, he became so occupied with his new training, she stood behind him. Not that

90

she had any mystical insight that something special was happening. She didn't. She had taken him to his first decathlon, and his second; they didn't appear special to her.

'I didn't know a thing about the decathlon,' she says. 'It was a non-event in England. Nobody knew about it, least of all me. I wasn't any more excited about that than his winning a 100 metres somewhere, because I thought it was a one-off thing. Fine, he's done great, he's too young to do any more, and that was it.

'I had no idea anything special had begun. I was pleased for him. I was thrilled for him, because it was something new he'd tried and he'd won. I met all the boys, and they were great guys; they'd made a fuss of him. I thought that was really nice. And that's all I thought. I never thought it was the start of a great career.'

As far as she was concerned, the decathlon was something he had found that he loved to do, and she was happy to help him. Whether it was with clothes for school or a new pair of spikes for training, she managed. And when those demands began to outstrip her resources, she went to the Inner London Education Authority, getting him a little money to help with expenses.

Not until the following spring did she sense that something had changed. That was the end of May 1976, at the Olympic qualifying competition. It was there that a lot of people began to get the message.

That winter leading up to the qualifying competition was a good one for Thompson. The training with Longden was going well, and he was becoming more comfortable with the ten events. There were no decathlons, but there were track meetings virtually every weekend, and his progress throughout the season – the process of building toward the spring and summer – was satisfying. He won the 200 at the AAA senior indoor championships at Cosford in January. In March, at the AAA juniors, he won the 200, the long jump, and came second in the 60 metres and third in the shot put. He won the high jump and long jump in April in an Essex Beagles competition against the rest of Essex at Mayesbrook Park and, two weeks before the trials, again competing for the Beagles in a British League meeting, he won the long jump, was placed second in the shot and third in the high jump.

The trials were held in Cwmbran, site of Thompson's first three decathlons. Despite his steady progress over the preceding eight months, he was most cautious in his optimism. 'There was no talk about the Olympics,' says Thompson, recalling that spring. 'No serious talk. I was a bit young. I hadn't done many decathlons. I think most people thought I might be a flash in the pan, so there was no need to talk about it. The Olympic qualifying mark, remember, was 600 points more than I'd ever done before.

'I'm not saying that I didn't view it as a possible goal. A possible goal can be so far ahead of you that your chances of reaching it are about the same as jumping over the moon, but you can still dream about it. But if you're seriously attempting something, then you've obviously got a chance. At that time, qualifying wasn't a serious goal. Particularly not for the first decathlon of the year.

'I was just going there to see how things were faring. To do better than I'd done before. Even as I approached the 1500, it seemed far away.'

At the end of nine events, he was still 624 points under the qualifying score, which meant he would have to cover the 1500 metres in 4 minutes and 25 seconds, 6 seconds faster than he had ever run before. The other athlete in the competition with hopes of qualifying for the Olympics that afternoon was Mike Corden from Sheffield, and he had to run the race even faster.

Though the odds against Thompson were high, the competition contained elements which could work in his favour. First, nobody expected anything more than a respectable showing, which he had already accomplished by the time the 1500 started. Also, he had help from friends. Pan Zeniou was in the decathlon, and running in that very race. Just having him there took an edge off the tension. Snowy Brooks was in the race too, but his help was more active. He would be the rabbit, setting a pace during the first 800 metres to get Daley around the course in the required time, then dropping out.

He had moral support. His brother Frank was there, and his aunt. It is a race that Doreen Rayment remembers very well. 'I thought it was beyond his capability,' she says. 'I was right at the finishing line, down on the track. It's so informal at decathlons – there's nobody there – they let you walk around. I'd recently had a hip operation, and still needed a crutch. I remember hanging on the fence with one hand, and I had my crutch in the other hand.

'Every time he was going around I was timing him on the stopwatch. I was thinking to myself, "He won't do it, he won't do it. Yes, he will, yes, he will. No, he won't, no . . ." Every time he came past I was screaming at him to hurry up, hurry up. And on the public address, Tom McNab, the national coach, was yelling the both of them on [Thompson and Corden] – "C'mon boys, you can do it. Pick it up, pick it up." When he came up to the last 100 metres, he had something like 10 seconds left and I thought, "Oh, no, he can't." And he just put that little spurt on, and he got over the line and I looked at my stopwatch and he was about half a second inside the time. I just let everything go and sat down on the track.'

Frank was waiting on the other side, and he caught Daley as he came over the line, lowering him to the track. Then, after a few minutes, Thompson went over to his aunt. 'He gave me a hug, then went and got me a chair,' she recalls. 'Then I made a fool of myself as I always do and burst out crying.'

Thompson's time was 4 minutes and 20.3 seconds, 1 second behind Zeniou, who won, and just ahead of Corden, who finished third in the race and second in the overall competition. Thompson's winning total score was 7684, 34 points above the Olympic qualifying mark. Mike Corden eventually qualified later in the season, but injury kept him from competing in Montreal.

All attention that day, however, was on Daley Thompson, with everyone at the track descending on him. Officials, athletes, everyone fought to congratulate him. 'Even if I didn't know something special had happened,' says Mrs Rayment, 'that told me. Those officials. They're all stiff-upper-lip, keep-to-the-regulations, and there they were, screaming at him.'

Even Thompson, by nature quite reserved about such matters, remembers the day with genuine fondness. 'It was a good race. I was really happy. I'd made good progress. And I qualified. I was surprised. Most surprised. Oh, it was obvious – I figured . . .' He stopped himself in mid-sentence. 'Naw, I never figured anything. I didn't know. I was doing something new. I still didn't have a clue what I was doing. It was all just really good fun. The fact that I was doing well made it all even better. I only just knew what events followed what events. I didn't have a clue about the tables. It was all so new. But it was so good.'

7

A Hint of Glory

The International Olympic Committee was no more successful in keeping the 1976 Games safe from the world of reality than it had been in the past. While there was none of the terrorist horror that plagued Munich four years before, the Games in Montreal were far from carefree.

Tight security was described as a 'collar of iron' by the IOC's executive director, expenses left the city of Montreal with a $1000 million debt, and the ever-present shadow of political domination strained the myth of a sports utopia. Worse was the politics. First the Canadians barred the team from the Republic of China, then the Africans, protesting against the New Zealand rugby team's tour of South Africa, boycotted at the last minute, sending 441 athletes back to eighteen countries.

But once the Olympic flame was lit, several hundred fine athletes got down to business. And some of them were brilliant. Nadia Comaneci, the tiny fourteen-year-old Rumanian gymnast, not only overshadowed Olga Korbut's performance four years earlier, but surpassed all of her predecessors by achieving seven perfect scores and winning three gold medals. Lasse Viren, the Finnish policeman, duplicated his double win of 1972 in the 5000- and 10,000-metre runs. And Bruce Jenner, the American, scored personal bests in his first five events, and went on to break the world decathlon record by 76 points.

One delighted witness to this spectacle was Daley

Thompson, who was seventeen when he arrived at the Olympic village that summer, becoming eighteen on his second day of competition. He had, in all, worked only sixteen months on his new event, usually in relative seclusion, competing mostly in front of a handful of spectators in southern Wales. Suddenly he was at the twenty-first Olympics, surrounded by the cream of the world's athletes, performing before one of the largest sports audiences in history, in person and on television all over the world.

'It was an unbelievable experience,' says Thompson, who became the youngest man to compete in an Olympic decathlon since Bob Mathias. 'I was able to walk around amazed at all the people I was rubbing shoulders with, people who, a couple of weeks before, I'd just been reading about, or just seen films of, whom I never thought I'd meet; people like Lasse Viren, or Olga Korbut or Bruce Jenner.

'I talked to everybody about everything they do. I picked up their schedules, everything they would tell me. Then I assessed it, to see what might be any good for me. I was like a little bit of blotting paper. I didn't miss anything.'

At the end of the first day's competition, Thompson stood in eleventh place with 4055 points, a respectable score that was aided by good showings in the shot put and the 400-metre run. But on the second day his inconsistency in the throwing events – especially a throw of 45.18 metres in the javelin, nearly 12 metres under his previous best – brought him down to eighteenth place. His final score of 7435 was 1181 points behind Jenner's world record.

Still, for a teenager taking part in his sixth decathlon, his first in front of so many people, it was not at all bad. Five other decathletes there didn't do as well, and another five failed to finish. It was a valuable education, watching during those two days such men as Nikolay Avilov, the Russian who had won the Munich Olympics, Guido Kratschmer, who would prove to be his chief rival

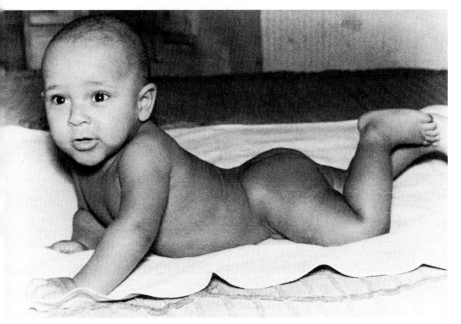

Daley at nine months: 'A terror from the minute he was born,' according to his mother

At sixteen months, he was walking and talking

At eight, on summer holiday from boarding school

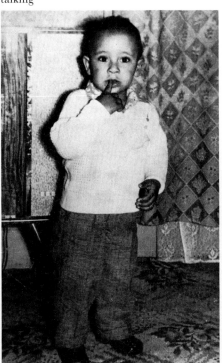

Above: With fellow students at Farney Close, aged eleven

Left: In the Farney Close jumping pit at fifteen: 'He used to dive over like Superman,' recalls his brother, 'head first'

Facing page:
Top: With his good friend, Bob Mortimer

Bottom: High jumping at the Commonwealth Games in Edmonton, 1978. Two days when nothing went wrong

Embracing his Auntie Doreen in the stands at Edmonton; her jacket carried the message 'DYNAMIC DALEY WILL DO IT'

Facing page:
In winning the Commonwealth Gold Medal, Thompson became the youngest decathlete ever to score 8400 points

Thompson looks on form again three weeks after the exultation of Edmonton, but here at Prague, disaster

Thompson crouches down after the
1500 at Prague

Long jumping to an Olympic Gold
Medal in Moscow: 'As long as I've
won,' he had said, 'I don't mind dying
the day after'

At a charity football match during the winter of 1979 in London, Thompson is the
preferred attraction

Above: The sprinter: power plus form

Facing page:

Top: With Guido Kratschmer in Bremen, Germany

Bottom: Mobility training with Pan Zeniou at New River Sports Centre, Haringey

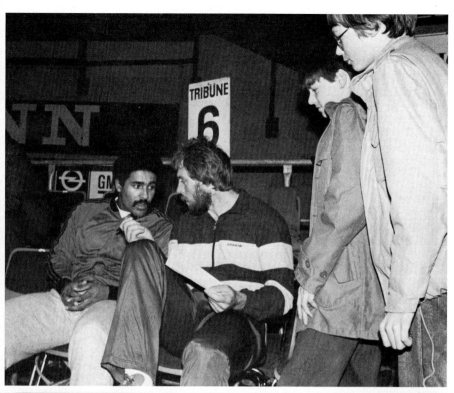

Javelin training at Haringey

Lecturing to athletes in Lagos, Nigeria

Training with Zeniou at Parliament
Hill during the blizzard of 1981

Richard Slaney demonstrating shot-put
technique in San Diego, 1982

Thompson stands amidst fallen rivals after the 1500 in Athens. Four years after Prague, sweet revenge

The Gold Medal at the 1982 European Championships, and a new world record

over the four years to come, and Bruce Jenner, who would raise the world record for the third time. Especially Jenner. Seven personal bests, capped by a 1500 in 4:12.6, a full second faster than his previous best. It was a farewell performance to be admired.

'If I were the kind of person to be impressed,' Thompson said years later, 'that would have impressed me. It was good. He looked relaxed and under control, rattling off one pb after another. One of those once-in-a-lifetime decathlons.'

While Thompson was pleased with his showing, the Olympics put the decathlon world into perspective for him. There were a lot of fine athletes out there, most of them functioning at a level much higher than where he found himself. He was close enough to be able to appreciate the difference between what he was doing and what they were doing. He could look at a man scoring 8000 points and respect what it had taken to get there, knowing well how hard he had worked and having an idea of what lay ahead. All around him were men who had their technique down perfectly in every event, who had done it all so many times that thinking wasn't required. He understood that, and he respected it.

What the experience did not do was intimidate him. 'The only difference between me and them was that my ability hadn't been developed,' he says now, looking back. 'I never felt that anybody there was so good that they couldn't be beaten. Nothing there was out of my reach. The only thing was, it was going to take time. I reckoned in four years I could be in the top six in the world, and so I could possibly have a chance for a bronze in Moscow. But in eight years, I could win. I reckoned in 1984, with eight years of work, I could win.'

That timetable, which many would have considered ambitious at the time, turned out to be modest. The first indication of this came later that summer when, after a month of competing in open events, Thompson travelled to Talence, France, during the first weekend of September for an international meeting.

It is a little unusual to have an international so soon after the Olympics, but this one had a particular purpose. It was intended as a showcase for Guy Drut, the Frenchman who won the 110-metre hurdles at Montreal and considered himself a good enough athlete all-round to challenge in the decathlon. In the end, the athletic world focused on Alexandr Grebenyuk, one of a group of fine Soviet decathletes. The talented but often injured Russian won the event with 8486 points, a European record. Disappointing though it was for the hordes of photographers, reporters and television cameras, Drut's debut was not a success. He never finished the decathlon, though he did last long enough to set a decathlon mark in the hurdles – 13.6 seconds, a record that still stands.

Thompson, who nearly missed the 100 because his plane was late – he actually changed in the taxi cab on the way from the airport – scored personal bests in four of the first five events, and went on to total 7905 points, a UK and Commonwealth record, coming fourth behind Grebenyuk and Gratschev of the Soviet Union, and Lahti of Finland, all much more experienced athletes.

It marked the beginning of truly world-class performances for the young decathlete, and a sprint of growth that had even his head spinning. After a winter of intense training, he began the 1977 season by coming third in the international at Götzis in May, behind Sepp Zielbauer of Austria and Fred Dixon, considered in the USA to be the heir apparent to Jenner. Thompson's total of 7921 represented a world junior record.

The following month he journeyed to Madrid for a four-nation encounter against Spain, Denmark and Italy. He produced outstanding performances in the vault, high jump, 1500 and 400 – his time of 47.4 seconds in that race was faster than the 400 winner in the British championships – to win, becoming the first Briton to pass 8000 points and the youngest man ever to amass that total.

'Madrid 1977 – me and Big Zeni,' recalls Thompson

fondly. 'It was good. I think it was Madrid – me and Zeni in the high jump. I improved four inches. It was nice. Boiling – nice and warm, it was. I went 8190, hand time.'

When Thompson visits an old decathlon in his mind, it is similar to a retired soldier remembering a battle. He zeroes in on the memory, calling back the feel of the track and the smell in the air, the progress of each of the events and finally the outcome. Madrid was a special victory. In the decathlon, 8000 is a major achievement. At that time only fifty-two athletes had ever scored 8000 points, and only fifteen had ever scored more than Daley Thompson did that June weekend.

Looking back to Madrid, he discounts any particular significance for him in breaking the 8000-point barrier: 'I was performing at a level that people were excited about, but (a) I didn't know 8000 from 7000; and (b) I still wasn't doing as well as I thought I could do. I thought it was good, but the important thing was that it was better than the 7921 that I'd scored before, and that's all I was ever interested in – doing better.

'I was really pleased with it at the time, but I just thought to myself, "Boy, I can do 8190. I can do 8300 next time." That's the way I always think. If I can do that with this rubbish, next time I can get it together a bit better.

'Even though every time I do it it seems to get better, I always think I can do tomorrow's *today*. I always think that. That was why, the next month in Sittard, I wasn't happy with 8124 electric. I didn't know in those days that it was better.'

Sittard is in Holland, where Thompson won his next decathlon a month later. The references to 'hand time' and 'electric' mean that the races in Madrid were timed by officials with stopwatches, which was common until then, and the races at the meeting in Sittard were scored automatically, by electronic devices, always the case in major competitions today. Electronic times are more accurate, and always slower than hand times. So while it appeared that Thompson had a less successful competition in Sittard than in Madrid, it was the more critical measurement of time that lowered his score, not his performance.

'I wasn't too pleased with the score from Sittard because it was less than I'd scored before,' explains Thompson. 'Intrinsically it was a better decathlon, but the automatic scoring made it appear worse. I didn't understand that then; coming up with a lower score meant no improvement to me.'

He finished that impressive season by leading a team of thirty British athletes to compete in the European junior championships at Donetsk, Russia, emerging as one of the UK's two winners. While his score of 7647 points was less than he had hoped for, the competition was a character-building exercise that could have been disastrous. Much farther from home than he had ever travelled, he found the atmosphere dreary, the food not to his liking, and his own concentration far from under control. His slim lead of the first day all but vanished in the rainstorm of the second, and, rattled by an uninspired hurdles and discus, and a vault that was 1.10 metres under his best, he retreated to his room – a clear violation of the rules – before regaining his composure, returning to the track and winning the gold medal.

As that 1977 season was coming to an end, Thompson was faced with a dilemma. For the preceding two years he had attended Crawley College, training whenever he wanted and using whatever education grants he could pry out of the system to live on. Still, getting by was tough. The first year he lived with Bruce Longden, and the second year he shared a flat with some friends from college. He ate wherever he could, at Longden's, at Bob Mortimer's house after training with the Beagles, or on the run, grabbing a sandwich and a carton of milk during the long train ride from one track to another. At weekends, of course, he stayed with his Aunt Doreen.

The second year at Crawley, training took up more and more of his time, anywhere from five to seven hours a day, with extra time for travel. He began resenting the time demanded by his classes. By his own admission he was enrolled because it provided the only opportunity for him to continue to train and live, but even that was becoming an unacceptable arrangement. And it was going to get worse as he approached the 1978 decathlon season. He would have only nine months to prepare for three major competitions: the international decathlon meeting in Götzis in May, the Commonwealth Games in Edmonton in early August, and the European championships at the end of that month in Prague.

He felt he could do well in all of them – even win – but he would have to train harder than he ever had. What he wanted to do most was just train, worrying about nothing but the season. England has a system by which 'elite athletes' receive money from the Sports Aid Foundation, through the British Amateur Athletics Board, for training and maintenance. Unfortunately, Daley Thompson was not considered elite enough.

'We applied for aid in 1975,' recalls Thompson, 'but they turned me down. Bruce tried to tell them I was going to be good, but they wouldn't listen. We scratched up some money to go away that winter for training. Two weeks in Nice – I enjoyed that. Me and Doreen paid my share.'

Midway through 1977 a flurry of rumours surfaced about his going to America to attend universities from Massachusetts to Arizona or California. Much of that probably began when Dave Hemery – gold medallist for the UK in the 400-metre hurdles at the 1968 Olympics and, by 1977, track coach at Boston University – invited him over for a visit that Easter. Nothing came of the invitation – 'It's pretty cold there in winter,' Thompson said of Boston – but then during the summer he received a grant under the Colgate Palmolive Sports Scheme, which was later that winter followed by a small maintenance grant through the BAAB, the latter, according to Thompson, enough to keep him in milk.

The sum of all that help was still not a lot to live

comfortably on, but it was enough to permit him to devote himself full time to preparing for the coming season, which he did by working even more intensely with Longden, and competing all winter and spring in open events, at Woodford, at Crystal Palace, at Cosford and of course at Mayesbrook Park in Barking. On one Saturday in May he travelled to Perry Park in Birmingham and competed in six different events, winning four of them, then showed up at Crystal Palace the next day to compete in two more in a Southern Counties AAA match.

He opened the decathlon season the following weekend in Götzis at the international meeting there. The year before he had come in third; this time he was second, raising his point total 327 points to 8238. He had actually led at the end of the first day, scoring 4300 points, but Guido Kratschmer, the West German who had won the silver in Montreal, overtook him on the Sunday with an impressive total of 8498, the fourth highest score recorded at that time.

There was no let-up. He returned home to compete in five different meetings during June, then began tapering off in July for the Commonwealth Games, scheduled for Edmonton, Alberta, the first weekend in August.

The situation in Edmonton was close to perfect for Thompson. He was in good health and he had been training hard. Fifteen separate meetings since the first of the year – thirty-eight competitions in various events, in which he finished first fifteen times and second eleven. In a British League meeting in Southampton midway through June, he had won five of six events he entered. He was ready.

The Commonwealth Games are not like other internationals. They are all 'family'. Everybody speaks English, and many of the athletes know each other. And if the crowd normally in attendance wasn't comforting enough, Thompson had his own rooting section. His Aunt Doreen was there, and Pan Zeniou. Most important, Zeniou.

Thompson, on the right company: 'It was great that Zeni was there. I've always found that when I go to a decathlon I need somebody to chat to, just so it's like normal, not a big occasion. It has to be as close to normal as possible, because that's when you perform best, when you feel at ease.

'It was funny about Zeni. He wasn't selected for the British team. We left and went to Edmonton, and he was at home. He never told me he was going to represent Cyprus. Zeni comes to the airport, says goodbye to me, and that was that. I said, "Zen, I'll see you when I get back. Sorry you couldn't come," and all that sort of thing.

'So we get to Edmonton, and I'm at the disco that evening. All of a sudden somebody comes up and puts his hands over my eyes – you know how people do. It was Zeni. I said, "Zeni, you having a holiday? Zeni, what are you doing here? Has somebody got you in for the day?" He said, "No, no, I've come to compete." I said, "Zeni, c'mon." But after half an hour I believed him. I was really happy. We had a good time, and he did all right. I think he came in third or fourth.'

During those two days, nothing went wrong for Thompson. Even the wind was at his back. (A little too much at his back, actually. The allowable wind in a decathlon is 8.9 m.p.h., which made the 5 m.p.h. assistance in the 100 permissible, but the 11.2 in the long jump enough to earn his score an asterisk.)

He sprinted to a personal best of 10.50 in the 100, and followed that with a long jump of 26 feet 7¼ inches, or 8.11 metres. Only one other Briton, Lynn Davies, the 1964 Olympic long-jump winner, had ever gone farther, but Thompson's mark was a Commonwealth Games record.

His shot, high jump and 400 were all strong, despite the wind, so helpful earlier in the day, turning against him towards the end. He finished with 4550 points after five events, not only a personal high for him but 253

103

points ahead of the pace set by Jenner in his world-record performance in Montreal.

But the decathlon is a two-day event. Decathletes tend to excel on one day or the other, depending on where their individual strengths lie: Jenner, a good thrower and middle-distance runner, had better second days. Thompson, a natural sprinter and jumper, has better first days. And while his second day in Edmonton was not a disaster, it did expose his youth and inexperience in the technical events. He hit nine of ten barriers in the hurdles, threw only 41.68 metres in the discus, then struggled to respectability if not brilliance in the final three events. All in all, a good two days' work, totalling 8467 points, making him the youngest man ever to score 8400 and ranking him among the four best decathletes of all time.

'It was all right,' says Thompson with his customary control. 'I was going there to perform my business. I'd been working hard, training to achieve certain goals: to run 10.5 in the 100, to long jump 25 feet, and so on. I go into every major competition with that in mind. It didn't get to be special until I was finished. I was pleased, but I wasn't surprised.'

His performance may not have surprised him, but the reaction of the world did. Suddenly, the word was out, and a flood of attention soon followed. That attention didn't even wait for the competition to be over or the final score registered. The BBC was on hand for an interview after the first day and *Sports Illustrated*, the American weekly sports magazine, followed his progress closely.

Thompson was more than up to it. An apt performer under normal circumstances, he dazzles before camera and microphone. He was witty for the folks back home, and properly modest for the US audience. ('I'm still a first-day performer,' he told *Sports Illustrated* writer Kenny Moore. 'Give me time and I'll be a decathlete.') Then there was the action back at his room, urgent messages from universities and colleges all over the

United States, requests for him to call back, reversing the charges, to speak with track coaches and athletic directors who had visions of his wearing the colours of their colleges in the coming track season. It was all an abrupt change and, at the time, very pleasant.

Two years later, in a paperback book called *One is My Lucky Number*, Thompson commented about his initial reaction to the sudden burst of attention:

Overnight everything changed dramatically. From then on I had to get used to people recognizing me in the streets, waving to me from their cars when they happened to draw up next to me at the traffic lights, and coming up to me in restaurants.

I loved all that – and I still do. I think that secretly this kind of adulation and fame was what I had been working for all my life. The recognition, the autograph hunters – it's great. It occasionally gets me down when the kids follow me around from shop to shop, but most of the time I really enjoy it. At first it seemed too good to be true.

I say that the Commonwealth Games victory changed people's attitude to me overnight but actually it happened even quicker than that. Immediately after the decathlon had finished I went out with Auntie Doreen (who, as ever, had come out to watch me) and some other close friends for a slap-up meal complete with champagne and all the trimmings. We ran up a big bill of several hundred dollars and yet when the time came to pay, the manager wouldn't hear of it. It's on the house, he said, and congratulations. That was my first taste of what stardom was about.

The commotion lasted throughout his stay in Canada, with attention from the international press, free lunches and free dinners, more phone calls from universities, and even a few track coaches making their pitch in person, offering apartments, cars, expense money, and even a maid.

Back in London, the tempo picked up. Thompson talks about cab drivers offering free rides in exchange for his autograph, and his phone ringing constantly with newspaper reporters looking for interviews or just a quick quote, some piece of the newly crowned national hero.

'People were different,' he recalls. 'It was all very strange. Nothing had changed, not really. I'd been promising that sort of thing for a year or two and I wasn't surprised. But everybody was looking at me like I was this rising star.'

His newly won fame made the smattering of publicity he had known before resemble obscurity, but there was little time to enjoy it. The European championships – the biggest meeting of track and field athletes outside the Olympic Games – were scheduled for Prague in just three weeks. Important as the Commonwealth Games were, Czechoslovakia was infinitely more prestigious. The finest athletes in Europe would be there. Among the decathletes, Grebenyuk of the Soviet Union, Siegfried Stark of East Germany and, of course, Guido Kratschmer. If Thompson were going to prove that Götzis and Edmonton were not flukes, he could not wish for a better field.

Again, he was ready. More than ready, he was eager. In athletic parlance, he was sky high. He was getting the feeling that nothing could stop him. Nothing, and nobody. 'You've got to remember,' he says, 'I'd got there and I was just twenty years old. Three weeks before I'd scored the seventh highest score of all time. That's unreal, especially when you never thought it was going to happen. So you think the next time you try, God knows what you're going to do.'

Keeping up that sunny attitude once he arrived in Prague was not easy. He found the city drab and unpleasant; the dormitories small and dark. Things didn't improve when he reached Rosicky Stadium early that Wednesday morning in August. 'It was really rather oppressive,' he says. 'Everybody's a lot more serious than at the Commonwealth Games – there's a bit more at stake.

'It was a difficult competition for me, because I didn't have anybody to talk to, nobody at all. Nobody there speaks English. There were sixty or seventy of us who had come over, but they weren't out there when I was, so they might as well not have been there. I was lonely, and I was cold. It was bloody miserable. It was raining – I had to change four times a day. It took three hours for the high jump, and it was pissing down. It was just horrible.'

Even with the long list of talented decathletes in the meeting, Thompson reckoned the only man he had to beat was the West German. And when Kratschmer showed up with a heavily bandaged right thigh, amid rumours of injury, his confidence grew. The two men were in the same 100, and when the gun sounded Kratschmer ran only a few strides before pulling up in pain. Thompson never looked back. He streaked for the tape, breaking it with his arms raised in an instinctive gesture of victory.

There was a stir of disapproval from the crowd at what they considered unsportsmanlike behaviour, a reaction shared by neither of the rivals. In a race of 100 metres, one had won and the other had lost; nothing else had taken place. Kratschmer, himself a fierce competitor, understood.

With his primary opponent out of the competition, and despite the poor conditions, Thompson continued to build his lead throughout that first day, until by nightfall he was 288 points ahead of his nearest challenger.

Along with a lot of other people, he felt the decathlon was his. From the first-day coverage of a major London newspaper, dateline Prague, 30 August:

Daley Thompson is poised to become tomorrow the first British athlete to win the decathlon title in the 44-year history of the European athletics championships. At the halfway stage tonight he is well ahead of the second man with a total for five events of 4459 points, and his major rival is no longer in the competition. No Briton has previously won any medal in the European decathlon, let alone the title, the nearest being Peter Gabbett's sixth place at Helsinki in 1971.

107

The article followed with a quote: 'This is hard work, not like Edmonton where it was simply fun. But if I can keep it up tomorrow, I reckon the gold medal is mine.'

But then came the second day. He ran a sluggish hurdles, nearly half a second slower than Edmonton, then followed with a personal best in the discus. In Edmonton he had cleared 15 feet 9 inches in the vault, and had been vaulting a full foot higher in practice during the intervening weeks. But he had to settle for 13 feet 9½ inches on that day, as on his second attempt, while he cleared 14 feet 5¼ inches, a gust of wind blew the pole against the bar, knocking it down.

In every event, Grebenyuk had been gaining ground. And while Thompson threw the javelin 196 feet 2 inches, another personal best, the Russian's strength was in his throwing, and his javelin reached 222 feet 3 inches, moving him into the lead for the first time in the two days. It was a moment that Thompson still remembers. 'After the javelin, I didn't want to run any more, I didn't want to run the 1500, because if I wasn't going to win I didn't really care. I didn't really want a silver. I certainly didn't want a bronze. I didn't think I had a chance at any of them. I just wanted to go home.

'Then I met Brendan Foster. He'd won a European gold in 1974, and a bronze in Montreal in the 10,000. He was going on in a couple of hours, and he was just sitting, chatting to me. He told me something I'll remember all my life. That is to go home with the silver is better than going home with the bronze; it's better than third place, or fourth. So if you can't take the gold, take the silver, because you'll only feel even worse if you come all this way and have nothing to show for it. So I got myself together and I went out there and ran.'

Thompson and Grebenyuk were in the same 1500, with a British victory by 8.5 seconds required to close the gap. The gold was still within reach. But there was more than one Russian on the track that evening, and it was clear from the start that they would be running as a team. With Grebenyuk taking a quick lead, team

mate Yuriy Kutsenko was left to handle the challenge.
He ran in front of Thompson, blocking his path, and
once even knocked him to the ground. Thompson, forced
to the outside lane, eventually passed his obstacle and
went on to defeat Grebenyuk, but by a margin of only
1.6 seconds. He knew the instant he crossed the line that
it wasn't enough. He sank to the wet surface and stayed
there, crouched down on his haunches, staring into
space.

'I ran all right,' he said later. 'I didn't run fast enough,
but, considering where I'd been, or where I was coming
from, I ran all right.'

The British protested at the behaviour of the Russians,
but were told their action came too late. Even if upheld,
Grebenyuk was not directly involved in any interference
and it is unlikely he would have been affected. The one
most affected was Thompson, and in such a penetrating
manner that his entire being was laid open as it had
never before been.

At the time, he preferred to deal with the pain the
way he deals with most things personal: he kept it inside.
His aunt knew, of course, for he raged around their flat
like a man facing his own destruction. The meaning of
what had happened was that catastrophic to him. He
had finally found a role in which he wish to be for ever
cast – as a winner – and that quickly they were trying
to take it from him.

Few people outside his immediate circle knew what
he was going through. From many of his closest friends
he hid the truth. They saw he was upset, saw him
remain at home for a few weeks, then return to train with
renewed commitment, working harder than ever. For
those who knew Daley, it was easy to assume that was
all of it.

Years later, having come more to terms with the loss,
he felt he could discuss it. If ever there were any question
about how badly he needed the decathlon and needed
to win, his reaction to Prague answered that question.

Daley Thompson, on defeat: 'It was devastating. You

don't know how devastating it was. It's impossible to put it into words. My vocabulary doesn't have enough words to describe what I was feeling. It would be different if we had more scope in our language – like Eskimos have twenty-seven words for snow, different words for different types – but we have only one. Depressed, abandoned, lost. Worse than that.

'It wasn't that I let other people down. I don't care about anybody else. I didn't give a damn about anybody else. Man, it was me. I let myself down. I hadn't performed well. I don't usually get depressed, so when it happens it affects me. And I was depressed, really depressed.

'I've never considered suicide, so I don't know for sure, but I would think that's how people feel. Suddenly it's worse than it's ever been and you can't imagine it getting better. And even if it did, it wouldn't make any difference, because you just don't care. Nothing matters, because you lost. You knew you were going to win, and you lost.'

One might consider his reaction extreme, his grief excessive. He was, after all, only one month past his twentieth birthday, an age when most of the men who are going to be great decathletes are just learning their event. Three weeks before, he had come within 150 points of the world record, and there, at Prague, he had been placed second in a field of the finest decathletes in the world, many of whom were recognized as possessing superior talent.

None of that carried any weight with Thompson. Expecting victory, he had lost. But while he grieved about it at the time – he still considers it the worst day of his life – in the years that have followed he has gone back over the experience, picking it apart, analysing what occurred, evaluating it, trying to discover what happened, and why. He doesn't blame the weather; everyone competed under the same conditions. He doesn't blame the tactics of the Russians; that's part of the game. He doesn't blame his training; he was ready.

110

'What was at fault was me: I just didn't perform the way I should have,' he has said. 'It wasn't a physical thing – it was mental. I got carried away. Lack of self-control. I was in a hurry. But that's one of the things you have to learn when you're young. Slow down, take your time. You'll get there just as quickly if not faster.

'It wasn't that Kratschmer pulled up lame and I thought it was over. Even then, that young, I knew I still had to do it. There were still three others who were supposed to be better than me. But something happened. Maybe, with Guido out, I tried too hard. You can do that, try too hard. That's just immaturity. People who aren't old enough don't accept what they are told. They have to learn it.'

What he did, in the months and years following Prague, was take that defeat and treat it as if it were another part of the decathlon, one more event to be mastered. A lesson to be learned along with all the others. 'It was a good learning experience. I know that it will never happen again. The value of it is that I have learned to prepare myself for whatever comes up. I do, now. I don't want another Prague.' One lesson, judging from his growth since Prague, well learned.

8

Winter of the Phantom

The realm of international decathlon competition is mysterious. Men train for long and arduous hours, alone or in small clusters at various points around the globe, near their homes, or congregating at the local training facility. They test their progress in open meetings wherever they can find suitable, accessible competition: a 100-metre race at this meeting; a high jump competition at that meeting; long jump, shot and vault at another.

This plan is forced by necessity. While there are many track and field meetings in an average year, major decathlons are few. Two or three in an Olympic year; about the same every second year between. The odd years are leaner. So while runners and throwers and jumpers may challenge their rivals at every stop along a busy international circuit — as often as two and sometimes three times a week during the height of the summer season, should they choose — decathletes see one another infrequently. But although they may only meet once or twice a year, the time spent together is intense. Not the batting of an eye in which most athletes warm up, run their race and leave, but two full days of competing in one event, lying around and waiting for the next, then getting up and competing again.

As a result, strangely personal relationships develop between competitors sharing crucial times with perhaps the only other people who can understand what they are doing and why. After these encounters, each man returns home, often thousands of miles away. A few short days of intensity, then nothing but distance. During the off times, they keep in touch through hearsay and snippets of information culled from the international sports press, through such magazines as *Athletics Weekly* in England, *Track and Field News* in the United States, and whatever newspapers may carry an appropriate story or stray line of print, a name and a number in tiny agate type under a heading called simply 'Results'. So-and-so ran 10.30 in the 100 in France; somebody else vaulted 17 feet in Houston.

Through this strange kingdom late in 1979 moved the shadow of Daley Thompson. Though he was just twenty-one years old, a child in terms of the decathlon, his was the name most often mentioned. Though he had never won a major international of world-class significance, it was generally accepted that, come the showdown in Moscow, he would be the man to beat.

My first meeting with Thompson was early in December of 1979. We had agreed to meet in the mid-afternoon of the day I arrived in London. At that point in his schedule, he said, he would be at the indoor training area of Crystal Palace. I got there a little early, to look around.

The Crystal Palace national sports centre was built on the grounds and still carries the name of Joseph Paxton's masterpiece of architecture, constructed for the Great Exhibition of 1851. It had stood on eighteen acres of Hyde Park, but the agreement was that after the six-month industrial exhibition ended the park would be returned to its original state. So the glittering gem of glass and steel, 1800 feet long and 400 feet wide, had to be moved. A high ridge was selected at Sydenham, south of London, and in 1854 a new and somewhat enlarged Crystal Palace was opened.

The site of festivals and conferences, it was immensely popular, but it was also extremely expensive to maintain, and became more and more run down after the turn of the century. One night in 1936, fire broke out. Flames, visible for twenty-five miles around, soon consumed the building, and by morning nothing was left but rubble.

It was on this site in 1964 that the sports centre was opened. The only remaining vestige of the old Palace are the two artificial lakes, the great terraced lawn in the rear, and, here and there, life-size sculptures of prehistoric animals that once adorned the grounds.

Today the centre is the setting for most of the UK's important outdoor track and field meetings; it serves as the hub of sports activity of the many clubs, schools, organizations and local individuals enrolled in its various programmes. The 17,000-seat stadium has a football pitch of beautiful manicured grass, and an encircling track with a modern, artificial surface. There are other outdoor areas for football, hockey, cricket and tennis. The indoor facilities include three pools, courts for badminton, handball, basketball, squash and all manner of exercise and weight training. These indoor areas are well lit and well heated, with showers and changing rooms, a cafeteria and beverage and snack bars for the general public, plus private rooms.

But the indoor athletics area, the only place for serious track and field training in bad weather, is abysmal. It is a makeshift construction under an elevated walkway. It is long and narrow, poorly lit, poorly heated, and it leaks. Even when it is not raining, inexplicably, it leaks.

It was a little after two o'clock when the man I assumed was Daley Thompson arrived. There was not much doubt in my mind. The indoor area is virtually unused at that hour during the week, and I was one of two or three people there when this lone figure, dressed in shiny blue warm-up pants and a red windcheater, both bearing the familiar Adidas stripes, came in.

He seemed smaller than I had expected. That was partly because of the setting. Seeing him from across the long, dimly lit room, carrying his athletics bag full of shoes, he resembled just another athlete. Maybe a little more spring to his walk, a greater sense of familiarity in the way he looked around for a recognizable face, as if he were walking into his own living room, as if the area were his. Jaunty, self-assured. But he didn't seem terribly unusual, not then. He was a black athlete, with a close-cropped Afro and a thick, black moustache. In the United States he could have been one of several young athletes; in England, he could only have been Daley Thompson.

I stopped him and introduced myself. We walked together to one of the conference rooms on the second floor of the main building, where Bruce Longden was involved in a coaches' meeting. It was not quite over, so we waited outside. There were no chairs; we sat on the floor outside the closed door.

Sitting with him for the fifteen or twenty minutes until the meeting broke up, I got a much better sense of his physical presence. He wasn't terribly tall, a shade over 6 feet, but he was extremely broad across the chest and shoulders. Later, watching him train, stripped down to shorts and running shoes, I would see the development of his upper body, his shoulders and fore-arms, and his thickly muscled thighs and hard, rippled calves.

But it wasn't his size or physical condition that held my attention as we talked. It was his bearing, his sense of himself. There was, of course, that poise that comes with an accomplished athlete, a person who is proud of his body and his control of everything physical concerned with it. But there was more. That poise extended to what he said, and the way he presented it. He was at ease with me, at ease with the situation, right from the start.

We talked about my impressions of England and about the time he had spent in the United States – during the previous winter and spring he had made the first of many training visits to California. We talked about American foreign policy, and he asked me about the Iranian hostage crisis that filled the newspapers. It did not take long for me to realize that he was doing the interviewing and I was doing most of the talking; not the arrangement I had in mind.

We began talking about sport. Not the decathlon; not

even about participating in athletics events. About being an athlete, and dealing with the public, sportswriters, officials and fans. He talked about what they all expected – demanded, actually – and how little responsibility they were willing to assume. At that point, it was journalists he was referring to.

He began to parody some of the worst offenders. ' "Oh, yeah, what events do you actually do in the modern pentathlon? Is it still fishing, and riding and stuff?" It's happened, you know. I was once stopped at Heathrow, film crew and everything, and this reporter started talking about the pentathlon. If they can't do their homework, I can't be bothered to talk to them.'

In that first conversation, and in those that followed in the nearly two weeks we were together, it became clear to me that he was at one of those exceptional stages where athletes occasionally find themselves, especially those who are destined to go on and flirt with – or even achieve – some degree of greatness. That time comes after the basic groundwork is laid and the athlete has proved to himself how good he is, and before the rest of the world has found out and the pressure begins to build.

It was, in fact, the perfect time for him. The ghosts of his past were, if not laid to rest, at least comfortably out of sight, and he was able to enjoy the present while concentrating on the future. He had, in his own way, dealt with the disaster at Prague. While memory of the loss still plagued him, still on occasions snuck up on him and ruined an afternoon or even an entire day, he had succeeded in placing it in some historical perspective, along with the other pains in his earlier life. And as was the case with so much of that pain, he even managed to use it to his advantage. Like getting into a sprint stance before the hurdles, or starting the approach for the vault at the wrong mark, he had made a mistake, and he had recognized that mistake. And, as the good learner he is, a mistake recognized is a mistake corrected. Never again would he think any competition over before the end of the final event.

His success in that 1978 season had substantially altered his life. The British athletics establishment that had ignored him two years before now viewed him as a figure worthy of serious attention . . . and even a little support. Not the pittance they'd given him early in 1978, but enough money to use as a base for living, with extra money for training, for equipment and trips during the winter, away from the cold of England and into the sunshine of the South of France, or wherever else he wanted to go. For the first time he had money in his pocket to buy food whenever he was hungry, to go to the cinema if, after a day's training, he was not too tired to hold his head up and enjoy it.

As he began to acquire national recognition – the Sportswriters' Association voted him their Sportsman of the Year at the end of 1978 – accompanying fringe benefits stretched his money from the Sports Aid Foundation. Hertz gave him their Number One Award, which earned him free use of a car. And although using the fame he had gained through athletics to endorse products for money would at that time have cost him his amateur status, sponsorship was another matter. That is the condition under which an athlete receives goods or services from a company, but not cash, to help him get by. Thompson's sponsors in 1979 were British Caledonian Airways, who flew him throughout their system without charge, and Baxters Butchers, who gave him free meat each month.

Even the overtures he turned down ended up working to his advantage. After winning the Commonwealth Games, he had received over twenty offers from colleges and universities in the United States. He decided to visit half a dozen. 'Texas-El Paso, San Diego State, Oregon, or maybe Oregon State,' recalls Thompson of the seven-week tour, differentiating between the two universities in Oregon by the fact that one had a blue synthetic track. 'They didn't want much from me, but I decided I'd rather stay home.'

117

Just how serious he ever was about the possibility of attending any American university is highly questionable, but he did enjoy the tour, and came away with a favourable impression of California weather, San Diego State, and Joe Briski, the university's assistant track coach at that time. So favourable that, while he did not want to attend classes there, he did think it would be a nice place to train in winter. He introduced Briski to Richard Slaney, who ended up winning a track scholarship. That was 1979, and Thompson has been going over there every winter since, to visit Richard and train.

These various developments combined to make for Thompson the kind of life he had wanted all along, one in which he would be able to concentrate on training and studying for his event, without anything else getting in the way.

As I discovered during those two weeks, very little got in the way of his work. The decathlon was the lens through which his entire world was viewed. He didn't stay out late. He didn't smoke, he didn't drink, he didn't experiment with drugs – he did nothing that could impede his progress. Even the question of where he slept each night depended on where he trained that day. Because he worked so much with Bruce Longden, and Longden lived in Crawley, Thompson stayed during the week in Crawley, in a spare room in the house of Jack and Adrienne Pyke, who had no relationship to him other than that he had once gone out with their daughter. At weekends he went home to his Aunt Doreen's, as always.

But in 1979 even that changed. Her tiny flat had long since proved hopelessly undersized, and they looked for a small house. The place on which they settled was in Worcester Park, a compromise location between his training sites and her work in Kensington, and considerably closer for Thompson than the old flat. On those occasions when he was too tired to travel at the end of his training day, he would sleep where he was, at the home of a friend or, if it were Crystal Palace, at the dorm there. In the back seat and boot of his car he kept

118

enough clothes for several such nights, along with the training shoes and discuses, the rolls of tape, the spike extractors and anything else he might need in the course of an average week.

Trying to keep up with him throughout one of those weeks was tough. I was staying at a hotel in central London, and met him each day at Crystal Palace or the leisure centre in Crawley. I was determined to follow him every step of the way, from morning to night; that was what we planned that first afternoon at Crystal Palace. I would begin the next morning, which was a Friday.

He began with a forty-minute run through Tilgate Forest near Crawley. It was one of those really cold days, damp and grey, with thick fog that resembled rain suspended in the atmosphere. In addition to his tracksuit, he ran in a stocking cap and gloves. After that, he worked on his shot and discus for an hour and a half at the leisure centre. It was eleven o'clock by the time he started, and while the day had brightened up, there was little warmth in the morning light. He had to keep the steel shots in a bucket of hot water just to warm them enough so he could hold them.

He broke for lunch, then returned to the weight room at the centre at 3.30 for an hour and a half of lifting. It was nearly five o'clock when he finished, and we drove the hour trip to Crystal Palace, where he had planned to work on his hurdles with some of his friends.

The rush-hour traffic was horrendous. We did not arrive till well past six o'clock, and found the indoor area dark, the hurdles put away and his friends gone. I did not mind at all, and was happy to call it a day. He insisted on looking around. We tried the snack bar upstairs, walked through some of the changing rooms and finally, in the weight room, found Snowy Brooks, Dave Baptiste, Steve Green, and two or three other athletes. Brooks, as usual, was leading the group in exercises, pushing the younger men to see which would be the first to drop. Thompson joined right in.

After that day, I gave up my plan of shadowing him from the moment he woke up and contented myself with meeting him at Crawley or Crystal Palace around eleven in the morning. Crawley was mostly for throwing – discus, shot and javelin – and for the centre's weight and exercise room. The indoor facility at Crystal Palace was where he worked on his high jump, long jump, vault and hurdles. He also ran on the track outdoors, and sometimes up the hills of the adjoining property.

The amount of time actually put in working, not even counting travel, was staggering. Ninety minutes of nothing but throwing. Loosening up, the mental and physical preparation. The concentration on technique, breaking each event into components of form. The actual throwing and, while retrieving, thinking about what was done before and what would come next. Then doing it over again. Over and over and over – the right arc, the right point of release, arms and legs and body in the right place at the right time. Break for lunch, a little rest, then come right back and start again for the long jump and vault, for hurdles and high jump, then round it off with a little weight lifting before dinner.

Every one of the skill events has its own technique, its own pattern that must be followed to perfection, the right move at the right time. It must be learned first, the way one learns a lesson, but then it must be carried beyond that level. An athlete thinks while learning; there is no time to think in competition. By then each action must be part of him, the way he blinks his eye to avoid an offending insect. It is what Thompson was talking about when he marvelled at the decathletes in Montreal. Then, he was still thinking, still learning; they had made it part of themselves. They had done it all so many times that each sequence of moves for each event came automatically. That is how it must be. For any great athlete, it must be automatic. And that is why the decathlon takes so much time to challenge at a world-class level.

'You never think, not when you've got it,' says

120

Thompson. 'You just do it. That seems impossible when you're starting. It's like when you try a new drill for the pole vault. The first six months that you do it you can't do anything that you're supposed to, because you haven't got any time. But once you can do the drill you can do three in the time that you couldn't do one. At that point, you've got it. But of course, all you've got is a little piece.'

For most of the technical work, Longden was there, watching him vault, watching his work with the shot, passing brief comments. 'You released a little early on that one.' 'You need a little more height.' Rarely any more, and hardly ever any kind of exchange between the two. Coach, standing, hands in his pockets to keep warm, watching. Athlete, watching himself from inside, then acting, over and over. All very serious.

For the non-technical work, the pattern was different. The running, the weight lifting, the exercising, the stretching, those labours he carried on mostly by himself, as he had done for years. He and Longden worked out a schedule of what needed to be accomplished, and Thompson followed it to the letter, rain or shine, cold or hot, fit or tired. He used to joke that the great joy of being an athlete was that he never had to train if he didn't want to. He could, if he wanted, just lie in bed for the day. In truth, he never did. The one time that I ever saw him leave early – he was ill, and running a high fever with cold sweats – every one around him was amazed. They'd never seen him quit that early for any reason; it was about six in the evening.

By that winter he was working out more with 'the boys' than he ever had before. Nobody's training schedule was quite as rigorous as his, so there were still many hours in the morning spent alone, but by mid-afternoon the group had begun to assemble. Pan Zeniou, working at his job in recreation, had the most flexibility, and was usually the first to break loose. Later in the afternoon, and during the weekends, Thompson would usually connect with Dave Baptiste and Snowy Brooks, and sometimes two or three others.

That was the best of it for Thompson, the times when the work became fun. What was being accomplished was no less important than the endless hours of striving for technical proficiency under the silent scrutiny of his coach – strength and stamina are crucial ingredients in the decathlon formula – but they came through an easier route.

Those times came in the exercise room, with Brooks leading the callisthenics. They came during sprints, with Baptiste challenging his friend to cut yet another hundredth of a second off his best time. They came with Zeniou while building stamina, charging around the track for 300 metres, walking for recovery, running another 300, walking some more, over and over. And never was there silence. From Brooks's taunting during the exercise to Zeniou's urging of a faster pace during the 300s, the game that could be lost only by not working hard enough was always loud and sweaty and good, all of it played against the blaring background of Baptiste's huge radio. The Police were the hot group that winter, and every fourth song seemed to be 'Walking on the Moon'.

'They make it bearable,' says Thompson. 'It's definitely lonely work. It's definitely hard work. Sometimes it gets to be too lonely and too much hard work. You can't do it in isolation. I've spent so long in isolation – just with Bruce, or totally alone. Every single morning, every single afternoon, every single evening. Terrible. Not terrible at the time, but when I look back on it, I don't know how I stood up. I wouldn't change it. It makes you what you are, but I wouldn't want to do it again. It's better now, and they help make it that way.'

Just thinking about his little band brought a smile to his face. 'Baptiste takes the hardest work and makes it seem normal. He makes it all good fun, because nothing's serious to him. With Snowy, you've always got to do another one. Whatever happens, there's always

122

one more to be done. He never lets you off with what you think is enough. He comes in and says, "We're gonna do six times this or that." As soon as you've done the six, he says, "Well, fellas, you've got ten minutes left, so you might as well go another two."

'Zeni makes me laugh. He always tries to make things humorous. And he's genuinely dedicated to me. He always knows when enough's enough. He'll always give me an honest opinion. Like if we're running 300s, I'll say we'll run 'em in 40 [seconds], and he'll say 38 would be better. Or if I say we'll run six, he might say four'll be better. I can always rely on him to be honest. And Richard, well, Richard's always there. Even when he's away, he's always there.

'I can rely on all of them. When I think I can't do any more, they tell me I can. They believe I can do anything.' The natural question arises: when you feel you don't want to train any more, isn't it possible it's time to stop? As Bob Mortimer might say, you can do too much. 'I don't think so,' says Thompson. 'Bob and I differ there. His own experiences have made him over cautious. Training is the only way you can guard against defeat. There is no way of assuring you won't lose, but by training – all you can – you at least know you're getting everything out of yourself that's there.' The lessons of Prague, over a year later, remain vivid.

Still, things were going very well. In decathlon terms, he was young, his education nowhere near complete. While he was performing at the level of an experienced, battle-tested athlete, he had spent barely five years with his event. His best performance to date – the Commonwealth Games – was noteworthy as much for his weaknesses as for the fine score he achieved despite them. By his own assessment, he was still picking up points in his speed events, and was years away from making the breakthrough that he anticipated with maturity in the more complex skill events. Looking ahead towards that growth, he had a coach to help him with his progress; together they had mapped out a strategy.

There were aspects of that strategy that confused experienced decathlon watchers around the world. After Thompson's fine showing in 1978, great things were expected of him for the new season. But he did not show up in Götzis in May, or at a three-nation meeting against France and Switzerland the following month in Dole, France. People wondered why, but Thompson and Longden were resolute.

'We are working on a five-year plan to reach a peak at Moscow next year,' Longden was quoted as saying in the London press when asked about the inactivity. 'Therefore it is essential this is a quiet season.' Privately, Longden was not that happy with his athlete's schedule of meetings. While Thompson was competing nearly every weekend in open events, and doing very well, that is not the same as putting ten events together in one decathlon. The coach saw that as a problem.

'This is where he and I differ,' Longden said. 'I personally would have liked to see him in two decathlons this year. He didn't want to do any. The happy medium was one, and that one was nearly a success. But it wasn't a success.'

The one was the German decathlon in Flein, the last weekend of July. Thompson was ready, but his vault poles were lost by the airlines, not an uncommon occurrence. He completed an excellent first day, hoping they would arrive by the second, but they never did. He tried without success to vault with borrowed poles, then withdrew without finishing. ('Trying to vault with borrowed poles,' he says, 'is close to impossible.')

Thompson dismissed the notion that competing in many lesser decathlons was the best way to prepare for major competitions. Winning the Olympics, he said, was his only goal, and open events were the best way he knew of readying himself. 'I didn't think there was any need to do more,' he said, 'as long as each individual thing was going well. I have enough confidence in my own ability to put it all together. For my club one Saturday I did seven events in three hours, and all of them were good. Something like 6.9 in the high jump, 10.5 in the 100, 25-something for the long jump, about 16 feet for the pole vault. Admittedly, those are my best events, but it does indicate everything was going well.'

It was a mild conflict, but that Thompson should feel strong enough about his own instincts to act on them indicated, even then, that at twenty-one he was beginning to assume more control of the physical, external elements of his life. He had, since first meeting Longden and taking up the decathlon, willingly assumed the role of student, accepting that he had so much to learn that he did what he was told.

The new attitude of self-determination exhibited itself in many areas, most noticeably in his relations with the press. His excitement with his early success led him to talk openly with reporters in the beginning. And the reporters loved it, for Thompson was never at a loss for words on any subject. 'Quoteful' was how he described himself. 'Good copy' is the journalists' term. However, his natural exuberance and confidence came across as brashness and arrogance. Once that public character was set, it seemed to have its own momentum. But Thompson reassessed many things after Prague, and his image in the press was one.

'I haven't been giving many interviews,' he told me that December. 'There are some things you should talk about and some you shouldn't. Sometimes I've talked too much. It doesn't mean anything. Regardless what you say, you've still got to go out there and do it, so there's no need to say anything. You might as well just get on with it.'

It wasn't that he totally stopped talking to sports-writers. He talked to some, those who had, in his judge-ment, accurately reported what he said and, just as important, bothered to learn something about the deca-thlon. But what was in evidence during those final months of 1979 was his caution about what he did say

125

in public. And whatever was written – however it came out – rarely did he have any comment.

One afternoon, after a morning's work in Crawley and a late afternoon session at Crystal Palace, he went upstairs to have a Fanta and some sweets in the coffee bar by the pool area. He was sitting at one of those little tables with Brooks, another athlete and me when he was approached by a reporter from one of London's major dailies. It was obviously someone he knew well.

The man pulled up a chair from the next table and began to chat about training, asking how various things were going and making specific reference to a couple of meetings in which Daley had competed that winter, one at Crystal Palace and another at Cosford. Then he opened up a large envelope he had brought and unveiled a chart of all Thompson's decathlons up to that time, with the individual scores of each event neatly written in little boxes. He went over it for a few minutes, then went back into his envelope and pulled out a manuscript he was preparing for publication. It ran about ten pages, and he asked if Daley would read it. He agreed.

Thompson read the pages quickly, handing each to me when he had finished. After checking with the writer, I too began to read. It was well written, a feature on Thompson the Man, scheduled to run just before the Olympic Games began in July and intended to introduce Daley Thompson to whoever might be curious about this enigmatic character, one of those 'What's He Really Like' pieces. What interested me most was the lead, which first referred to his generally accepted façade – the brash, arrogant, cocky athlete – then declared it was no façade at all. That's the real Daley.

It was a clever introduction, which opened up to nine pages exploring Thompson's public and athletics personae, colouring in that image that had become so popular in the English press. By the time I was finished Daley was already discussing the piece with the writer. More accurately, not discussing it. He just nodded, indicated that he thought it was OK.

Later, when we were alone, I asked why he fostered such an image so fervently, even to the extent of not correcting it when he was given such an opportunity. 'The thing is,' he said, 'you really can't change what people think, no matter what you say.' There was a note of resignation in his voice.

'It started after Edmonton,' he said. 'People started coming up to me and telling me how much I'd changed. Well I don't think it's necessarily me that's changed. It's people's attitude towards me, and the way they think I should be acting. People expect me to be brash and arrogant, or whatever, so they come and speak differently from the way they normally would.

'And sometimes, when someone comes to you with a certain attitude, you give them what they expect. You have to, don't you? You have to play up to people. It's like most things; it's a show. People expect it, so you give it to them.'

Controlling his relations with the press was still an easy matter in 1979. First, there was Bruce Longden to act as a filter for all requests for time and interviews; second, the international world of athletics had yet to attach a face and personality to the exceptional scores he had been compiling. At home, while he was certainly a recognizable enough figure, there was little comprehension of the calibre of athlete Thompson was, even then. There was no suspicion that in years to come he might accomplish important athletic feats. The big names in England were Sebastian Coe and Steve Ovett, men blessed not only with marvellous talent and skill, but with the good fortune of competing in events comparatively easier to understand.

That condition seemed to please Thompson. 'It's just fine,' he said when asked about Coe's grabbing most of the big headlines. 'He deserves it. Nobody else knows how hard it is to hold three world records at the same time. [In the span of six weeks that summer, Coe had broken the world records in the 800 metres, the mile, and the 1500 metres.] So let the press write about him

127

for the next seven months, and leave me alone to train. Let them all leave me alone.'

They did. With visitors at a minimum, there were few distractions during that winter before the Olympics. So long as he remained inside his little enclave, he went unbothered, even unnoticed. More than anything else, that was a testament to people's ability to get accustomed to anything. In the working-class, mostly white and reasonably conservative community of Crawley, Daley Thompson was a figure who stood apart. And late that December, when Slaney came back from his first term at San Diego State and began throwing with Daley at the leisure centre, the pair was hard to miss. At least twice a week the two friends would go into Crawley for lunch, usually eating at their favourite hamburger joint in the middle of town. Walking along the pavement together, they were quite a sight: Thompson, 6 feet 1 inch, black, with Afro and moustache, dressed in blue warm-up jacket and pants; Slaney, 6 feet 8 inches, close to 300 pounds, dressed all in bright red, the combination of size and colour making him appear to glow.

When he did venture outside, it was with the understanding that there was a good chance he would be recognized. About ten days before Christmas he went into London with Bob Harris, a journalist friend, and Harris's son Dominic, so that the boy could visit Father Christmas at Selfridge's department store. It took an entire afternoon. The itinerary included lunch at McDonald's, a stop at the cinema in St Martin's Lane specializing in Walt Disney films for a showing of *The Aristocats*, and finally, a walk up Regent Street to see the lights and visit the toy department at Selfridge's. The streets were so crowded it was hard to walk, and the line at the store stretched all the way through toys, into the next department. It took only about ten minutes there for the attention to shift from Father Christmas to Daley. First came the whispers from the children standing closest to him. 'Isn't that Daley Thompson? That *is* Daley Thompson. Is it really?' Word spread from child to child, the commotion growing louder and louder, until Daley was surrounded, pencils and scraps of paper having materialized from mothers' purses.

Nobody screamed or pushed; it all fell well within the limits of good manners. For Thompson at the time it was new enough for him to be flattered. And best of all, when he had had enough, he always knew he could retreat into his training, where he would be safe.

That was what made 1979 so good – he was taking control on all levels. He could spend most of his days working, take time off with the people he liked best, and he was bothered by few outside pressures. Even the romantic interest in his life, Patricia Quinlan, a close friend since they were both students at Crawley College, had come to understand his commitment so thoroughly that she accepted his long hours of work and his need for rest when he was not training.

Thompson realized how good his situation was, and he defended it. Anything that threatened the balance between work and relaxation he dismissed. That included appeals to his social conscience: pressures that, for some, might have been confusing. Since Thompson is both a highly visible celebrity and black – a rare combination in the UK – he was approached repeatedly by civil rights groups in the hopes of enlisting his support. In most cases, their requests were turned down.

'It's the old thing about climbing mountains,' he was fond of saying when the subject came up. 'You can only climb one at a time.' Off camera, he would say, 'They only want me because I'm famous, and you can't get famous by attending all that kind of rubbish. The only way is to do my bits and pieces. I'm no good to anybody if I don't win.'

There was no anger in his voice. Just a clear understanding of what his life is about. He knew even then that he had reached where he was by winning, and promising to win more. Once he failed to win, everything he had fought for would vanish. That is the hard and simple reality of life in the world of sport. While most athletes know it, it means something different to each one.

While I was still in London, Thompson was to be a guest at the annual dinner of the Sportswriters' Association, the same group that had, the year before, named him their top sports personality. It was on a Sunday evening, and the gathering point was the home of a television producer. Late in the afternoon the guests began arriving. They sat around the living room, drinking and talking until it was time for dinner.

Minutes before they were to leave, a sportsman showed up, his agent in tow. He looked tired, with half-moon-shaped shadows under his eyes. He said that he had just come in from Heathrow, having been on the Continent for some commercial venture that had kept him up most of the previous night. He apologized for being late, and asked for directions to the bathroom so he could clean up. When he left the room, someone said something about how he was running himself ragged, trying to meet commercial obligations.

'I see what happens to athletes who get all tied up with making money,' Thompson said later. 'It changes them. I've got to keep myself happy for a few more years. I've never been so happy, doing what I'm doing, and to keep myself happy is to carry on what I'm doing. I might like an Aston Martin or a Porsche – anybody would – but I don't need one, and that's what it comes down to.'

He seemed to have tapped in early to the athlete's love of his game and his desire for perpetual youth through it. It is the kind of insight that usually comes later in a career. You see it on faces of ageing athletes around the world as they try to get old bodies into shape. They want one more season, just a piece of the dream they had when they began. Somehow Thompson recognized the dream early, and realized that it is never too early to begin keeping it safe. Even the example of Bruce Jenner in America, having become rich through television and films since his retirement in 1976, failed to sway him.

'I don't want to do anything now to cut this short,' he said. 'I want it to go on for as long as possible. When I'm thirty-eight or forty I'd like to think I'm still bumming it around tracks, doing it just for the sake of doing it. A lot of people will be talking about me, saying, "God, he's still here. We all thought he was going to pack up and become a film star, but he's still bumming around tracks, still being a pain in the arse." That's what I want people to say.'

That was the way he talked in 1979, as if he were a man who could see the rest of his life stretched out before him and liked what he saw. He had a schedule of goals he wanted to reach while working for the three months in the sunshine of San Diego, a training pattern he would follow. He would return to England early enough to begin preparing for Götzis. There he would begin the sharpening process that would bring him to a peak in Moscow in July. Moscow was the big stage. There is where he would break the world record, and lay to rest any confusion about his ability.

'I think I'm the best decathlete in the world,' he confided to me then, 'but Moscow will be proof for them. You've got to prove it to them. The Olympics is the place to do that.'

Looking at the world decathlon situation at that time, it might not be so clear to an outsider why Thompson was so confident. After all, he had not completed a decathlon since September 1978, and in that one he had come second. In the intervening season, some respectable scores had been registered by men who would also be in Moscow. Siegfried Stark, the East German, had won the European Cup with 8287 points. Jürgen Hingsen, the young West German, had scored 8240. The best score of the year, not surprisingly, was recorded by Kratschmer, who won the West German championships with 8484 points.

None of this impressed Thompson. His vision was

clear. 'Winning in Moscow is the most important thing in my life,' he said. 'I think about it all the time. I'm impatient. I want to get there and do it. It's like looking forward to going to a good movie. You can't wait till you go, especially if it's a good show. And this is going to be a good show.

'July 25 and 26. I fantasize about those days and how well I'll do. The day after doesn't mean anything to me. I'm not up to that yet. I'm only up to the last day. I've only got as far as the 1500. I might die when it's over, but that doesn't matter. As long as I've won, I don't mind dying the day after. Ten minutes after. Just give me enough time to savour it, ten seconds down the home stretch.'

I asked him if, conceivably, somebody else at the games might have a chance to win. He smiled. He knew better than I what had been going on in the world of the decathlon during the past season. He also knew that after London my assignment took me to Germany to see Kratschmer, a man whom he respected and with whom he had, over the years, developed a genuine friendship as well as an active rivalry.

'There's always a chance,' he said wryly. Then, more seriously: 'Don't tell Guido anything. Don't tell him anything about what I'm doing. Let him wonder. Let them all wonder.' I promised, thinking to myself what a strange request it was. Then I recalled an incident that occurred earlier in my visit, while he was working with weights in the power room at Crawley. I had my camera out and was shooting while he exercised. At one point, while he was pressing a particularly heavy weight – and having trouble with it – he stopped me from taking pictures.

'Please, no pictures while I'm lifting,' he said when he had returned the loaded bar to its stands. 'I grimace. People shouldn't see me grimace. They'll think I'm not invincible. I can't have that.' Cute, and at the time I laughed. But more than once during our time together he had requested that I not discuss exact details of his

132

training, and especially not report on times run and distances thrown or jumped in practice. Not until the following week, when I was in Germany, did I realize how serious the secrecy was. Once there, it did not take long.

There are many centres for the decathlon around the athletics world, the common attraction being a good coach and a good training facility. For years in the United States, the most respected name has been Sam Adams, head track and field coach at the University of California at Santa Barbara. The Polish decathlon coach is Andrzej Mankiewicz, in Warsaw. The legendary figure in West Germany has been Friedel Schirmer, who has been training champions since 1964, whether in Cologne or Dortmund, sites of his famous decathlon camps. Added to those names in the late seventies was Wolfgang Bergman, Germany's national decathlon coach, then in residence at the University of Mainz. At the time I was there in 1979 he was working with three decathletes each scoring over 8000 points.

His star pupil was Guido Kratschmer, the strong, quiet, almost shy farmer's son who would surely be Thompson's primary rival in Moscow. The two men had met in competition several times since 1976, with the German winning on those two occasions when both men finished.

He seemed to come out of nowhere in Montreal, beating the defending gold medallist, Nikolay Avilov of the Soviet Union, for second place, but his showing was a surprise only to the uninformed. In two other decathlons during that 1976 season he had scored 8265 and 8381 points, setting the stage for his Olympic performance.

For Kratschmer, winning a medal was part of an old dream. The seed was planted in 1964, when countryman Willi Holdorf won the decathlon in the Games at Tokyo. Kratschmer was only a boy of eleven then, living on his father's farm outside the tiny village of Grossheubach, working in the fields and in the stables. Holdorf's victory so inspired Kratschmer that he vowed to emulate it and, on his own, he began training every day after his chores.

'When I was sixteen a trainer came through our village, looking for young men to recruit,' recalls Kratschmer. 'Some of the people told him about me, this boy who was always running and jumping, so he came to see. He watched me and asked if I wanted to begin training as an athlete. I have been training ever since.'

By that December, Kratschmer appeared to be well on the way to fulfilling his childhood goal of winning in the Olympics. While he was a full-time student at the University of Mainz, studying physical education and biology, most of his time and energy went into the decathlon.

From his score of 8484 in the West German championships in June, he was ranked as the number one decathlete in the world. His four years of top-level international competition had earned him a comfortable place in the national athletic establishment. He was provided with living expenses from the German Sports Federation, with extra money for getting out of the cold winters. He had been to Santa Barbara, California, earlier that year and, as the crucial 1980 season approached, he would train for three weeks in Portugal, and relax for another week in Israel. And everywhere he went, he took his friend and translator, Karl Zeilch, because the Federation understood their athlete was a celebrity who attracted attention. Zeilch's job was to deal with that attention so Kratschmer could get on with his training.

The place where he did most of his work was the athletic sports complex called the University Sports Club, which is used at different times by the local sports club, the students of the university, and the German Sports Federation. It is a huge hangar of a building, 140 feet by 273 feet with a 30-foot ceiling, well lit, its temperature carefully controlled. It is large enough for several basketball games, 60 metres of hurdles, high jump, pole vault, discus and shot, much of that going on simultaneously. There are also weight and exercise rooms, and fully equipped showers and lockers. Just outside is a new track.

There were several decathletes training with Kratschmer when I visited, two or three younger Germans whom Bergman was bringing along, and Tito Steiner, the tall Argentine who, while attending Brigham Young University in the United States that year, had scored 8124 points at a meeting in Texas. They all wanted to know about Thompson, how his training was progressing. Some had been in Flein in July, and had seen the decathlon he never finished. They were impressed with what they saw, especially his times in the 100, 400 and the hurdles. And they knew some of his results from the summer, of his vaulting over 16 feet at Crystal Palace, and running the 100 in 10.8 seconds in August. The most aggressive interrogator was Steiner.

'This is December,' he said in confident English, 'how is he looking? We see scores of open events, but why does he not compete in a decathlon? And what about Flein? What happened there? The vault, it hurts him still. It is Prague, all over again. The great Thompson is flawed after all.'

Kratschmer's only question about Thompson during that first meeting was about his health, and that asked in the most solicitous manner. When we talked later, and over the next few days, it was about his life with the decathlon, what had happened in the past and what he wanted for the future. 'He expected to do well in Montreal,' said Zeilch, translating for his friend. 'Others were surprised, but he went there knowing he was good enough to come in first or second.'

Kratschmer actually speaks a relatively good though uneven English, but is more comfortable communicating through Zeilch, saving himself any possible embarrassment. That same cautious, nearly timid element of his personality was evident when I first met him. His manner, his behaviour, even his appearance reflected a man unimpressed with his own importance. He looked

135

like just another blond-haired, blue-eyed German student who was using the spacious gymnasium. Dressed in a warm-up suit and sporting a scraggy beard, he walked in as if he were visiting for the first time. Only later, when I saw him working out in shorts and T-shirt, was it clear what a marvellously conditioned athlete he was. Six feet 1 inch, 205 pounds, and solid. Huge shoulders with thick well-developed forearms, large strong hands, a broad chest, thick muscular thighs, and bulging calves.

His training was broken into ten sessions a week, each from an hour and a half to two hours long, so that all the decathlon skills received attention, with extra time devoted to weight lifting. And twice during the week he, his coach and some of the other decathletes headed out to the Gonsenheimer Wald, the forest just above Mainz, to run.

Workouts on the track could be chased inside by bad weather, not uncommon during the winter months in Germany, but the ordeal in the forest was carried on regardless. During the week I spent with Kratschmer the temperature hovered around freezing every day. And on the afternoon I accompanied him to the forest, it rained. Steady, frigid rain. But there were Guido and the others, after a full morning's workout, running their prescribed routes through the thick, slippery mud of the well-beaten trail. First they jogged 4 kilometres, just to loosen up, then commenced to run – flat out run – up a 186-metre incline, over and over, six times, with only the walk back down to recover their wind.

By the time the last run was over it was dark; I walked with Wolfgang Bergman back to where the cars were parked. Bergman, then close to forty, was in remarkable shape – he skipped none of the runs. As we walked he talked casually about training – he asked about the facilities Thompson used in England without inquiring about his schedule – and then, without my asking, he began talking about his student.

'It's very hard,' he said in firm if slow English. 'The training, it's very demanding. It leaves room for nothing

else. Guido's been at it a long time. He's had eleven
years of this.' He paused, and looked back at his team
of muddy athletes as they lumbered up the hill. It was
very dark, and it was cold and wet, and they all looked
miserable.

'This will probably be his last year,' he said, drawing
in a breath. 'He wants so much to win, but win or lose,
this will be the last. It's been a long time, and the
training is so hard. Necessary now, but hard.' By then
the others had reached the area under the trees where
the cars were parked. Bergman had business at the
university. Several of the athletes were going back to the
house of their trainer for a sauna. Zeilch asked if I
wanted to come along; there would be more of a chance
to talk, he said.

It was a good opportunity, so I tagged along, and set
up in the large sitting room of the cabin behind the
trainer's house. The sauna, I assumed, was in one of the
little back rooms. I went over my notes while the half
dozen athletes pulled off their muddy shoes in preparation for their post-run ritual. Suddenly I was aware that
the trainer, who was handing out towels, was standing
before me, two towels in his hands.

'This is for inside,' he said of the first towel, gesturing
toward the back. And holding out the second, 'This is
for out here.' I tried to explain that I did not really need
a sauna, since I had not been running in the cold rain,
but he was not listening. Nobody was listening. They
were all getting undressed. Rather than risk offending
my hosts, I did the same.

The thermometer inside the closet of benches and heat
read 90 degrees Celsius; the humidity, under 5 per cent.
It was hot, far too hot for me. But nobody said a word.
They just sat there on those white pine benches and let
their bodies absorb the dry heat. Fifteen minutes we
stayed in there, more than enough time for me to
appreciate what finely conditioned athletes they all were,
and how miserably uncomfortable I was.

After cold showers, we met in the sitting room, where,

clad in our dry towels, we were presented with huge
trays of whole sausages, all kinds of sliced meats and
cheeses, several kinds of bread and assorted rolls, and a
case of half-litre bottles of dark beer. I asked if this were
the usual snack, and was told not at all. This was special.
Today's run would be the last before Christmas.

There was a flurry of eating, and when it subsided to
slow, steady consumption of one beer after another and
a methodical picking over of the food, the conversation
resumed. At firs it was all in German but slowly more
and more English began to creep in. And soon, with the
help of my long-unused university German, I was able
to keep some semblance of communication going.

Thompson remained the central topic, and for the first
time Kratschmer began to enter in. Still talking through
Zeilch, he told me of his feelings for his rival, how much
he respected what Thompson had accomplished in such
a short time. The one decathlon Thompson had
attempted that year happened to be on his birthday, a
fact that came out that night after the competition when
all the athletes went out. Thompson had told me the
story, how Kratschmer, seeing him admire the German's
sweater, took it off and presented it to him as a birthday
gift. I told Guido how touched Daley had been by the
gesture.

'He is a very good person, as well as a great talent,'
Kratschmer said through Zeilch. 'It will be a great battle
in Moscow.' The conversation then switched to the
Olympics, first about the expected difficulty with tight
security and the terrible food, the problem of confronting
so many fine Russian decathletes on their native soil,
and then, taking the next logical topic, to the importance
of winning in Moscow.

'It is,' said one of the younger decathletes, 'the dream
of every athlete. You work and work, and it all comes
to those two days.' They talked of Hans-Joachim Walde,
a member of their athletics club, who finished third in
the Tokyo Games of 1964, then second four years later
in Mexico City. 'When you don't win,' said another of

the athletes, 'you think about all the time used. You ask yourself, what was it all for?'

'When you're just there to compete,' said another, 'then the thrill of being there is enough. But if you can be second or third you can be first. Then only winning is enough.'

There was a quiet, as if they were waiting for Kratschmer. In a moment he said something to Zeilch. 'You train and you train, every day for years,' said the interpreter, watching Kratschmer as he listened to every word. 'You do it because you love it, and because you know that is the only way to win. You want to win in the Olympics, because that is the best place to win. That is where the big game is. This is not America, where winning means money. Guido is not Bruce Jenner – he will not be rich from this. When the Games are over, he gets his degree and goes to teach. But if he wins in Moscow, his life will be different. He will have proved he is the best. That is what all this work is for, to know for yourself that you are the best.'

As the food on the tray began to thin, a fresh tray appeared, and more beer replaced the empty bottles, and the conversation became less and less understandable as it lapsed more and more into German. Periodically men disappeared from the table, heading back into the sauna, then to the shower, returning to the sitting room for more food. At some point, after a few of the younger athletes went outside to cool off after their sauna, I decided it was time for me to head back to my hotel. The following day I was scheduled to leave.

I got dressed, and the trainer agreed to drive me into town. Kratschmer walked me to the door, the first time he and I had been alone. As he said goodbye, shaking my hand, he said in nearly perfect English: 'Tell me the truth, how does my friend Daley train? Very hard?'

9

Pure Gold

On Christmas Day, 1979, the Soviet Union began flying military troops into Afghanistan in an effort to strengthen the staggering Communist government there. Within twenty-four hours some 6000 combat soldiers would take up positions inside that small country on Russia's southern border. By New Year's Day, a coup would end in the death of President Hafizullah Amin, a Marxist opposed to excessive Soviet influence, and 15,000 more soldiers would go in. Moscow saw the action as answering 'imperialist interference in Afghan affairs'. To the western world, it was invasion.

In his official response to what he termed a 'serious threat to world peace', United States President Jimmy Carter on 4 January announced a series of punitive moves against the Soviet Union, ending his speech with the following warning: 'Continued aggressive actions will endanger both the participation of athletes and the travel to Moscow by spectators who would normally wish to attend the Olympic Games.'

The impact of what came to be known as the Olympic Boycott was crippling. By 20 February, when it became official, the US government reported that twenty-three nations had agreed not to attend the summer Games. Many Olympic committees tried to cling to the independence supposedly guaranteed by the Olympic charter but were swept away by strong pressure from Washington. One was that of West Germany. The British Olympic Association, in blatant defiance of the express orders of the Prime Minister, Margaret Thatcher, did resist, and on 25 March voted overwhelmingly to go to Moscow. But they were a rare exception among the American allies. Every day, it seemed, another nation withdrew. Ultimately, nearly sixty nations would join the action.

It all made for a difficult winter and spring for athletes around the world. Many had no idea if their nations would join the boycott or not. Somehow they had to concentrate on their training while the controversy raged between their respective governments and Olympic committees.

None of this seemed to affect Thompson. If there was any doubt in his mind about the status of the British team, he never indicated it to anybody else, and probably not to himself either. If the image of a diminished Olympics concerned him, he kept it a secret. 'I didn't really care,' he said of the boycott. 'I didn't give a damn who was going. In 1956, when Switzerland and Spain and the others boycotted, nobody gave a damn, and in 1996, when they come around to look at the rolls of the winners in 1980, nobody's going to give a damn that America and West Germany weren't there.'

He competed at an open meeting at Cosford mid-way through February, winning the vault and shot put, then left for San Diego. He trained there for two full months, returning to England in time for the British League meeting at Wolverhampton, his last preparatory competition before the big international at Götzis. At that point, mid-May, he was in perfect shape to begin the sharpening process for the Games in July. Everything was on schedule.

'My plan was to break the record during the Games,' he recalls. 'To aim for something four years in advance, for everybody to know what you're aiming for, is the hardest thing you can do in any kind of competition. Everybody has advance warning – everybody knows what's going on. It would have been the perfect thing, but that's not how it happened.'

Thompson admits he's still not sure how he happened to break the world decathlon record in Götzis in May,

141

instead of three months later in Moscow. 'Whenever I do a decathlon,' he says, 'I'm in good shape and I can do some really good things. I can generally foresee most of the things I'm going to do, but not this time. Where usually six or seven go well, everything was going well. And there I was, knocking on the door for the record.

'It was a good meeting. The weather was good, there were a lot of people there, all the best decathletes in the world were there, and I just happened to perform at 95 per cent of what I was capable of instead of my usual 85 per cent. The thing was, I wasn't pushing. I was just flowing through. I'd obviously been working hard, and it was paying off. It wasn't as if I was trying hard. I wasn't, till the end. The last couple of events were getting difficult. I was getting physically tired.'

He recorded a personal best in the high jump the first day, *en route* to a total of 4486 points, actually less than he had scored in Edmonton two years before. But it was the second day where his great improvement showed, as he scored pbs in the hurdles, vault and javelin. That left the 1500, and a running time of 4 minutes 26.1 seconds necessary for him to break the record.

Thompson had a friend in the race, an American named Mauricio Bardales, who was pacing him for the first 800 metres. Later, the compact decathlete – he stands 5 feet 8 inches tall and weighs 160 pounds – told Neil Wilson of the *Daily Mail* that for the first couple of laps Thompson looked dead on his feet.

'I shouted at him to make his move, but his body wasn't responding,' said Bardales. 'But that man is all heart. Finally I kicked him into action.' Thompson covered the final 300 metres in 46 seconds, crossing the finish line with a time of 4 minutes 25.49 seconds. Bruce Jenner's world record total was 8617; Thompson had scored 8622. On the clock, the difference is the equivalent of seven-tenths of a second in the 1500.

Thompson says he doesn't remember any of the details of the race. But the finish, that he'll never forget. 'It was crazy. I'm standing at the finish line, and I'm saying to every single person who passes me, "What was the time?" Unfortunately, everybody I'm speaking to is Austrian, and only speaks German. I've got no idea what anybody's saying.

'My coach is running around like a mad thing, as if he's just done it. Everybody I know is off – I can't see a person. I'm waiting for three or four minutes. A long three or four minutes. I'm getting my breath back, and I'm feeling really, really angry because nobody's talking to me. Everybody's really happy with themselves. The meet director's happy because he's just got a world record, and left me not knowing. And it's been difficult.'

There was a big party that night but despite his protestations to the contrary, Thompson isn't much of a party man. His preference was to call his friends back in England, have a glass of orange juice with the people at the meeting whom he felt helped him, and go to bed. 'I wanted to get over it, and I knew it wasn't going to be easy,' he says. 'When you aim at things and achieve them, it's kind of an anti-climax. It's a big let-down. Not that I was expecting fireworks. I don't know what I was expecting, but whatever I was expecting, that wasn't what it was.'

There was a certain amount of public excitement about his breaking the record. After all, it had stood since 1976. Banner headlines screamed from across the London papers: 'Daley Does It!' Charts explained to readers just how he'd done it, comparing his results in each event with Jenner's performance, and reporters called the house non-stop with request for interviews.

Also waiting for him upon his arrival in London, a cable from America:

CONGRATULATIONS. EVER SINCE THE DAY I MET YOU IN MONTREAL, I KNEW YOU HAD THE RIGHT ATTITUDE TO BE THE BEST IN THE WORLD. I KNOW YOU'LL WEAR THE CROWN WELL. MY WHEATIES CONTRACT IS UP IN A YEAR – I'LL GIVE THEM YOUR NAME. 9000 OR BUST.

FORMER WORLD RECORD HOLDER,
BRUCE JENNER

143

The '9000 or bust' comment referred to the scoring of 9000 points, the next plateau in the decathlon, expected by most experts to be reached some time around 1990.

It was soon after Thompson's return from Götzis that the real trouble started. He took a couple of days off to rest, as he always does, and then started training again. Back to the old schedule: Bruce Longden and Crawley in the morning; Crystal Palace in the afternoon, with Bruce or sometimes alone; evening sessions, usually at the Palace. But somehow, as he puts it, the old fire was gone. The fight, that aggressiveness that had been his edge, had abandoned him, and he didn't know what to do. Much as he tried, he couldn't get it back. He might have looked to Longden for assistance, but that had never been their relationship. Daley had always supplied his own desire; Bruce had helped with technique.

While he pondered the source of this mood that had fallen over him, he knew he could not surrender to it. Time was too precious. He might not have known what was going on in his mind, but he knew he had to keep working. He dragged every minute of training time he could out of his friends, especially Zeniou, and that was good. But he needed more. Fortunately, he knew where he could get it. He would go back where he had gone in the beginning, to Mayesbrook Park. The Essex Beagles were still there, and so was Bob Mortimer. He had never stopped competing for his club. Now he went back for their help.

'I was seeing quite a lot of him socially, at meetings,' recalls Mortimer about that summer. 'Actually, he started doing some training with us in 1979, but that summer he really came back into the fold. I think he felt he needed to run, needed to be pushed. This is a good place for that. He's got some good mates – they don't mind doing it for him.'

Over the years that Thompson and Mortimer have been friends, the coach has made astute observations about the athlete. He has watched his patterns of training, knows what he needs and when. He has learned to recognize the signs when Daley is ready to win. 'You can always tell what shape he's in by what he does before a decathlon,' says Mortimer. 'If he's ready, he'll show it that last time out. He hadn't run in Wolverhampton on 3 May 1980, which means he wasn't ready for Götzis on the 17th and 18th. If he's ready, he runs. In Götzis, he ran 48.08 in the 400, which is good, but it took a lot out of him. I'd say he did that on courage and guts. It really knocked him up.'

Mortimer calls Götzis a 'miscalculation'. He would have preferred that Thompson pick a few events during those two days – the 400 on the first day; the hurdles and vault on the second – test himself, then go for the record in July or August when he was really fit. 'The goal,' he says, 'was Moscow and the Olympics. He wasn't ready for that kind of test in May.'

Thompson responds: 'I'd spent four years trying to get there or thereabouts, and it doesn't really matter when it comes. If it's there, staring you in the face, the least you can do for yourself is attempt it. You wouldn't be much of an athlete if you didn't. You couldn't live with yourself.'

Mortimer shrugs in acceptance. It is not a point on which he could hope to move his friend. 'He's a competitor,' he says. 'He's got to win, no matter what. Even if it hurts him, he's got to win.'

By the first of June, what Thompson should or should not have done in Götzis in May was academic. There were less than two months to prepare for the Games, a period which according to Mortimer is just enough. 'He needs to know that he's not going well about seven weeks before a major meeting,' says Mortimer, 'and then he could build with his running. In June he wasn't going well at all. He was suffering. His groin was bothering him, his elbow was bothering him. But he came to work.'

He competed in five events at a meeting in Luton on 1 June. Pain and all, he placed second in the high jump and javelin, and first in the discus, the 4 × 100-metre relay and the 4 × 400 metres.

145

Two weeks later he suffered a setback, one over which he had no control. In a meeting in Bernhausen, West Germany – one to which he had not been invited – Thompson's world record was broken by Guido Kratschmer when he scored 8649 points. To this day Thompson swears he wasn't disappointed, insists that all records are made to be broken, and says that he sent off his congratulatory telegram to Guido in full heart. Still, in an already difficult summer, it could have been little comfort that the world record for which he worked so hard and which cost him so much lasted but twenty-seven days.

Whatever he felt about it in his innermost mind, the broken record seemed to give him a much-needed spur. He ran the 100 and 200 metres at an invitation meeting at Southampton on 22 June, and five days later ran the 100 at the Talbot Games at Crystal Palace. The next day he went with the Beagles to Edinburgh, competing in five different events in the British League meeting. Mortimer says he had to kick him off the track to keep him from entering more events.

'Even at Edinburgh he was suffering. He'd been suffering since Luton, but he ran. He's got guts. He ran for us at Haringey mid-week, then came back at the weekend to do the Southern Counties at Crystal Palace. He did quite a few events – 100-metre run, 110-metre hurdles, long jump and pole vault – and that's all in one day. That's good preparation. The next week he ran well at the Welsh Games. He'd done a 200, and he never does 200s unless he's ready.

'He came back the next day and ran very well for us in the British League at West London. He ran a bloody brilliant 4 × 4 leg [4 × 400-metre relay] and before that he did the 100, the hurdles, the vault and shot put. That's only a fortnight before the Games, and so he's running really well. By Moscow, he'd made himself ready, by the strength of his own will.'

He was, indeed, ready for Moscow. Whatever the cloud that descended over his subconscious, whatever

the pains that assaulted his body, he had managed to
deal with them, to accept them or block them out. As
Mortimer had said, by the strength of his own will, he
was ready. All that had gone before was forgotten.

'Now I'm happy,' Thompson said of his state of mind
a week before the Olympics. 'I've been waiting for four
years, and it's tomorrow.'

He arrived in Moscow about a week before the Games,
and spent that time close to the track. (Regardless of
how exotic the host city, before a competition Thompson
never strays far – physically or emotionally.) He
describes the atmosphere there as uneasy.

'Whenever you get to any major games apart from
the Commonwealth Games,' says Thompson, 'it's
always OK on the top, but very tense underneath. It's
worse with the Olympics. It's the most important time
in four years for these people. For some it's their first
chance; for others it's their last. For a lot it's their only
chance. Outwardly everybody's trying to be casual, but
they're really very tense.

'I messed around. I went down to the track and played
around, stretched a bit, threw the shot around, tried
some sprints. Nothing serious. If you haven't done it by
then, it's too late. Mostly I tried not to think of the
importance of what was going on, because as soon as I
thought about it I'd get all excited. I didn't want to use
too much adrenalin too soon. It was going to be a
difficult two days, and I wanted to save it.'

His competition began on the second day of the Olympics, and the night before he went to bed early, as is his
habit: about eight o'clock. Just how well he slept is a
question not even he can answer. He was keyed up, and
lay in bed thinking about home, about training with the
boys, about anything except the next day. Eventually,
he assumes, he fell asleep. But maybe not. Before more
than one competition he has lain there all night,
hovering between being asleep and awake, only to hear
from room mates in the morning of conversations he
never remembered. Since he roomed alone in Moscow,

147

he had no indication as to how that night passed. He does know that he was up and alert fifty-five minutes before his alarm was set to go off, which was 5 a.m. That left him plenty of time to dress, check everything in his bag and look over his spikes to make sure they were clean – 'Again,' he says, 'for the four hundredth time' – before going down to breakfast.

It is the normal pattern for decathletes to rise early on the day of a meeting. In order to get all five events in that first day, the 100-metre run has to start by 9.30, or ten o'clock at the latest. Anyone wanting breakfast has to eat two to three hours before that. After breakfast in Moscow, and the warm-up period which came later, all the decathletes were herded into a little room from which they were summoned for their respective races for the first event.

Daley, on the beginning of the Games: 'Right before you go out, when all the decathletes are in that one room, it's very strange. You know them all. You know how good they are and how bad they are, what their strengths are and everything, and you're deciding, if you're going to do it, you're going to do it now. It's make or break. When you get out there it's nicer than you thought, because you feel good within yourself. You've done the work for four or five years, and you know today's your day. You get out there and you run your race, and that's the start of it.

'The rest of it is a bit blurred. I don't remember much. I remember it was a nice day, and I remember doing well in my events, but that's all.'

That first day was dry if a little cool and windy, and Thompson broke on top with strong wins in the 100 and the long jump, and finished a comfortable fifth in the shot, then second in the high jump and first in the 400. Not a single personal best in the lot, but still a solidly balanced first day, giving him a total of 4542 points, eight behind his best day ever, at Edmonton, and leaving him 262 points ahead of his nearest challenger, Yuriy Kutsenko of the Soviet Union.

His total was also 56 points better than he had scored in Götzis in May, which meant he was within reach of regaining his world record. Kratschmer's margin had been just 27 points. 'It was a good first day,' recalls Thompson. 'Nothing went wrong, which is the essence of decathlon. It was a good night because I had a fairly good second day coming. I knew that. I'd always been worried about the second day because it had never been strong for me, but it's been getting better. I'm getting older; I'm getting stronger. I'm getting better. Actually I didn't sleep all that well. It wasn't a sound sleep. I was ready to start the second day right then. I was feeling tired outside, but good inside.'

Conditions on the second day were miserable. Rainy and cold, with gusting wind. The kind of day no athlete likes, the kind of day that drops scores and prohibits him from competing at the top of his form. It was also the kind of day Thompson refuses to use as an excuse.

'When I was warming up for the hurdles,' he says, 'a couple of the fellows fell over. I thought to myself, "One of the favourites in 1972 fell over. Jeff Bannister, an American guy. In 1976 one of the favourites fell over, Fred Dixon." And I thought to myself, "No way am I going to fall over." I was ready. I've trained in the rain. I've competed in the rain.'

He came second in the hurdles, running the 110-metre course in 14.47 seconds, a tenth of a second behind the personal best he'd registered in Götzis, and he was pleased. 'I didn't run to the limits of my ability,' he says. 'I didn't run flat out, which would put me on the edge of falling over. I was running within myself, in control. It was OK.'

He followed the hurdles with a passable discus – seventh – and a fine vault and javelin, considering the conditions. That left him with a massive lead after nine events, and still an outside shot at regaining the world record with a very strong 1500. 'I could have got close,' says Thompson. 'I could have run close. I think I had to run 4:17.9 or 4:18, better than my best. I know I could have run 4:20. It was possible.'

But he didn't do it. He did not even try. 'I'd kind of decided to myself that what I'd do was take the 1500 fast enough to win but slow enough to take in as much of the event as I could, to have it for myself. I ran fairly slowly, and every time they got too far ahead – I'd be counting the seconds, figuring the distance – I'd speed up a bit. I saw my aunt in the crowd; I saw my friends. Snowy was there. I even waved to them.'

Thompson finished tenth in the 1500, but it made no difference. The gold medal was his. He scored 8495 points, 164 points ahead of Yuriy Kutsenko of the Soviet Union.

There was some criticism back home of the way he treated that final event, the feeling being that if he were within reach of the record, he 'should' have gone for it. His compatriots saw the race on television, saw him looking around, waving, and some didn't like it. But none of them was in that decathlon; Daley Thompson was. He knew the conditions. And he knew what could be gained, and what was at risk. His decision indicated that the move towards control, begun early in 1979, was forging full ahead. This was truly his way.

'The record wasn't what I was there for,' says Thompson. 'I didn't care about the world record. If I'd been focusing my mind for five years on breaking the record, then fine, but I hadn't. It didn't mean to me what this did. And it isn't the little gold medal that they give you at the end. It's the two days that matter. I wanted to enjoy it, to have it for myself. And besides, this wasn't my last decathlon. It wasn't my last Olympics. If it had been, I'd have run faster. Twenty seconds faster, a minute faster. I don't know. But I'd have run faster, because that would have been it.'

It was late that night, nearly eleven o'clock, when the public part of Thompson's biggest day ended. It took that long to complete his victory lap – he insisted on decathlon team mate Brad McStravick running along with him – and to accept his medal in the nearly deserted Lenin Central Stadium.

The official part of the day, however, carried on into the morning. Every athlete must be tested for drugs when he's finished competing, and that is done by taking a urine specimen and having it analysed. Unfortunately, Thompson ate and drank very little during that second day. It took till nearly three o'clock for him to drink enough liquids so he could urinate and the Olympic officials could conduct their dope test. Only then did they let him out of their sight.

While much that happened during those two days remains locked away somewhere in a corner of Daley Thompson's mind, the very end he remembers: 'Three o'clock in the morning they let me out. The whole town's dead. Muggins wants to go partying, and the whole town's dead. The first time in five years I want to go out, right, and everybody's asleep. Every single person's asleep or gone.

'My dorm is just 250 yards from where they've been keeping me, but I take a little walk on the way back, because it's nice to be by myself. I haven't got these medical guys following me, like they have for the last five hours. I've taken the long way round, and when I get to my room I have a little screaming fit. I walk inside, see myself in the mirror, this silly grin on my face, and I start screaming. I've got my pillow over my head, and I'm screaming as loud as I can. "Yeaaah!"

'I wished I had someone to share it with. It would have been nice. I could've just sat there, me and Zeni, or Richard, or Snowy. I could've just sat there the whole night and gone "Yeaaah!"

'But I was alone, so I did it myself.'

10

The Honing of a Man

The Daley Thompson I found in England in the winter of 1981 was considerably different from the person I'd met two years before. That much was immediately perceptible; the exact nature of the change was complex. He was still a strong, confident and immensely gifted athlete. But something was different.

At first I thought it was just the passage of time. He was noticeably older, more mature. There was a calmness about him not present in 1979. Now, when he spoke of important matters, he was more firm, more direct, and the confidence he had always exhibited had deepened. Bravado had been replaced by a steely but quiet sureness, and he seemed to have acquired a new patience with the non-athletic world. In one early conversation, he joked about one of the benefits of winning the Olympic Games. 'It was nice to put to rest people's doubts about me,' he said. 'Not that I had any myself, but they had them. They always have their doubts.'

Truly, whatever doubt existed in the minds of the British people had disappeared. They still may not have understood the nature of the decathlon, but there was no question that Thompson was its star. His picture appeared regularly in the newspapers, and not only on the sports pages. He was a celebrity. Illustrated features publicized an exercise plan under the banner 'Daley Thompson, The Fittest Man In the World, Helps You Shape Up for Spring', and subsequent spreads discussed ideas on diet alleged to be his, and other tips for good living.

If you missed him in the papers, you could catch him on television. Soon after the Olympics, it was announced that Thompson would star in a ten-week series of programmes on Thames Television called 'White Light', directed at teenagers. The following season he was the host for a weekly sports show on the BBC.

In order not to compromise his amateur standing, an arrangement between the television networks and the Amateur Athletic Association was made in which the money was paid to the British Amateur Athletic Board, who would put it into a sponsorship fund to be used for Thompson's training expenses.

Through such ventures – there was also a weekly newspaper column for a time, and there were other approved projects – the money situation had eased considerably, and it promised to get much better. A proposal before the AAA would permit amateur athletes openly to endorse products, something previously forbidden. The money would be held in trust until such time as the athlete no longer wished to preserve amateur status. In the meantime, it could be drawn upon for 'training purposes', a term to be defined as loosely as the BAAB wished. If the need was for a couple of months of sunshine during the winter, that would be covered. If getting to the track for training required a car, that too could be justified.

The plan, in essence agreed upon by that winter, needed only final approval before going into effect in the new year. In preparation, Thompson had already signed with an agency to set up projects for 1982. 'We're talking about deals with camera companies, and international athletic competitions on television,' he said. 'All kinds of things.'

The media exposure, including his participation in 'Superstars', a television production in which athletes compete in sports other than their own, brought him more popular attention than his accomplishments in Götzis or Edmonton or even Moscow: stacks of fan mail, addressed to the television station or the newspaper, or

153

even to his home in Worcester Park. Most of it came from children, whose painfully formed letters often spelled out nothing more than their admiration. A typical message: 'Dear Sir, I think you are a marvellous athlete. Yours faithfully.' Others requested photographs, or bits of clothing.

The job of responding fell to Doreen Rayment. Every two weeks or so she would corner him in the living room and go over each and every letter. Those requesting a photograph received one of the colour prints supplied by Adidas, which Thompson would sign. Anyone wanting anything more, such as an old track shoe or discus, or a personal appearance or his support for any cause, almost always received a polite rejection. If, however, Doreen thought a letter deserved special attention, Daley would usually concur. She has always been his most trusted adviser.

Since I had last visited, there had been a dramatic change in the players on Thompson's personal athletics team. It seemed like a natural enough process, young men replacing their love of training with more conventional, usually less demanding pursuits. In some cases other athletes took their place – Greg Richards, who was on the junior decathlon squad in 1974 but dropped out, had returned and was training with Thompson – but mostly not. The ranks had simply shrunk. The only member of the old gang still putting in daily time was Pan Zeniou.

The source of instruction had also changed. Thompson's contact with Bruce Longden decreased steadily during the long summer of 1980, and they worked together not at all after the Olympics. Some observers were surprised at the change, but it is not unusual. Relationships between coaches and athletes – especially when begun so early in the athlete's career – tend to grow stale. The athlete goes on to another phase of his education; the coach begins working with a new prodigy. Longden's new student was Eugene Gilkes, nineteen years old.

The man on whom Thompson was relying for much of his coaching was Andrzej Krzesinski, a former Polish vault coach who guided Tadeusz Slusarski to a gold medal performance in the 1976 Olympic Games, and Wladyslaw Kozakiewicz to the gold in 1980. In the winter of 1981 he was working for the Borough of Haringey, and coaching at the New River Sports Centre. It was there that Thompson spent most of his time during the week.

Haringey was the natural choice for training head-quarters. It had everything he needed: completely equipped indoor area, with facilities for weight lifting, long jump, hurdles, high jump, pole vault, and a heavily netted throwing cage for training with the shot and discus. Outside there was the track, the infield for throw-ing, and hills for running. The manager, Sandy Grey, was happy to have him training there; the Haringey brochure proudly lists Thompson's presence alongside the centre's diverse activities. If there was a drawback, it was that Wood Green is on the other side of London from Worcester Park, nearly an hour's drive, but then Thompson was accustomed to travelling to work.

His usual weekday schedule that winter was to rise about eight o'clock and read for a few hours, then head over to Haringey and go to work, frequently not return-ing until ten or eleven in the evening.

His choice of early morning reading set the tone for the entire day. Scattered around the low bed in his room was an ever-replenished supply of books and journals on track and field, health and diet, exercise and training. Piles of them, from the most recent to others yellow with age. *Track and Field Dynamics*, containing chapters on axis of momentum and curves of flight. *Track Technique*, with articles on rear leg drive in sprinting, relay drills and training theory. More magazines, from the USA, Canada and England, containing articles on strength training, analysis of various techniques, and lots and lots of theory.

Some of the material was straightforward if dully

written, and generally easy to understand. Some seemed nearly unfathomable. An article in the February 1981 issue of Canada's *Track and Field Journal* was entitled 'A Research Review of Systemized Approaches to Planned Performance Peaking with Relation to the Sport of Track and Field', by Andrew McInnis, the national hurdles coach. It explored the various periods in a training cycle, with all the factors, physical and emotional, contributing to a performance, and ended by reproducing a diagram of these factors from an unnamed Soviet author. It resembled a plan for a nuclear power plant.

Thompson read it all, cover to cover, and had a way, without remembering titles or authors, of retaining those elements that he felt might be of value to him and his training. It was similar to his ability to recall the exact time, place and result of any competition he found interesting. Occasionally, when an event held some special significance for him, he seemed to be able to capture the moment in his mind. In a conversation about Bob Hayes, the record-holding American sprinter of the early sixties, he began talking about Hayes's performance as anchor man on the 4 × 100-metre relay team in the 1964 Olympics. Suddenly Thompson flew into an account. 'He was about 50 metres down with 10 metres to go: passed everybody; beat them by 9 yards, turned around and threw the baton at them. Take that, boys.' He stopped for a breath, then added: 'I've never seen that. I've read it so many times, but I've never seen it.'

He usually made it to Haringey by noon. Lunch consisted of two or three meat and cheese sandwiches picked up at a bakery in Wood Green, and a dozen swigs from a bottle of Tizer or some other soft drink, one of which seemed always to be in the back seat of his car. More often than not he ate in the car park of the sports centre.

While Thompson's primary interest in his new coach was to improve his vault, Krzesinski had experience with decathletes in Poland, and offered to outline a ten-week training programme. It was this programme that Thompson and Zeniou followed those weeks of

November and December. Each day contained specific exercises designed to get their bodies ready for the next stage of development, to be worked on in California that coming spring. Drills mostly, hurdling drills and high-jump drills, vault drills and long-jump drills, working with the medicine ball and with weights, running and jumping and hopping; building, building, so that muscles and tendons and nerves were ready for the technical demands to follow.

Haringey during weekdays in winter is little used. There might be a few classes from local schools during the early afternoons, but Thompson and Zeniou generally had the complex to themselves, to jog their mile or so on the outdoor track, work on their stretching or mobility exercises, then head into whatever was on the schedule for that particular day. November and December are the time for laying down a foundation on which the true skills of track and field are built.

As it grew later in the day, more and more people showed up at the centre, and whatever they did in the late afternoon usually required sharing the indoor facility with a basketball game or an exercise class. All of that activity took place in the front portion of the large, elongated, high-ceilinged building. There is also a rear portion, not quite so wide but very deep. This is where the throwing cage is, and the weight-lifting area, where the long-jump pit is, and where the hurdles are often set up.

By evening the entire complex would be packed. It was dangerous to walk two feet in any direction without being totally alert. In the front part, when it was not filled with six badminton games, plastic shuttlecocks flying about, Krzesinski might have the big pads pulled out, the standards set up and conduct a pole-vault class. That would still leave room in the near corner for Thompson and Zeniou to work with Jackie Jackson, their shot-putting friend, heaving the 16-pound ball against the wooden bench set up to protect the wall. Along the far wall, the women's heptathlon team might

157

be running the hurdles. That would still leave the back room, where men and women could be working out with weights, somebody could be throwing the hammer inside the rope cage, one group could be long jumping and another high jumping. I've seen all that, in one night.

While Thompson fully enjoyed the exclusive use of the building when he and Zeniou were alone there during the day, when it was full he accepted his role of being just another athlete, taking his place in line for the long jump, waiting his turn at the weights. Everyone there knows him and nobody would complain if he wished to monopolize some piece of equipment. But that has never been his way.

Or at least not usually. Sometimes, it is unavoidable. One evening about mid-way through December, after seven or eight weeks of working with the new schedule, a vault drill gradually became serious. It was a class of some twenty athletes, ranging in age from about ten up. They had all been working on basics for weeks and that evening Krzesinski was showing them how to handle themselves in the air. The exercise had the appearance of real vaulting. They were gradually getting some height, an elastic tape atop the standards marking the height achieved. Thompson was in line just like the rest of them, working on his technique. They lined up by size, which put him near the end.

At some point, after the best of the class had missed at his top height, Thompson asked if the tape could be raised. He had done no vaulting all season but apparently felt ready. The two boys standing at the base of the standards raised the tape to 4.30 metres, which he cleared easily. They raised it to 4.50, and he cleared that. At 4.70, he cleared.

By then the room, packed with athletes of all ages and levels of proficiency, was silent. Everyone stood and watched. He cleared at 4.80, and they all went 'oooh'. He had the tape raised to 4.90, and again he cleared it easily, and the crowd 'ooohed' again. The boys on the tape asked if he wanted it raised again, and he waved them off. 'It's early,' he said, and began helping the vault class take down the equipment.

They all stood there for a few seconds then, with a spontaneous buzzing, returned to their work. It wasn't that he had vaulted 4.90 metres – 16 feet 1 inch – that impressed them. It was that he had done it so effortlessly, so early in his training season and, as several noticed, while using a short grip on the pole. It was all so simple, so matter-of-fact for him, and so lovely to watch.

There was so much in what I saw that winter that seemed to say that Thompson was living a better life than when I had visited him two years before. He had succeeded in establishing himself as one of the fine athletes in the world. He had broken the world record, won his gold medal in the Olympics and was reaping the rewards. He was accepted as a star.

He seemed affected only in the most positive ways by all this. Instead of being defensive and protective of his new status, he appeared more at ease, less harried than before, as if he were no longer running to catch up with some public image. And while he was wary of hero-worship from strangers, he seemed to grow on the adoration of old, trusted friends. There was plenty of that.

People who had known him saw how hard he'd worked. Instead of jealousy, they showed appreciation, and for the old gang Thompson always had time, despite the demands of his training. I watched him spend an entire morning trying to help an old classmate from Farney Close through some marital trouble, and I accompanied him while he drove 111 miles in a blinding rainstorm to Birmingham to assist another old friend, javelin thrower and heptathlete Tessa Sanderson, who wanted to interview him for a local television show. And when it came to turning out in shorts and track shoes for the old club, Thompson was always there.

'Through all of this, he has remained a first-class club member,' says Bob Mortimer. 'He competes all the time for us, meetings, winter throw competitions, anything. He's always turning up, him and Slaney. And he's been very good about money. Nobody's ever asked, but he's always contributing something for equipment, things we really need. I'll bet he's given several hundred pounds.'

Thompson's relationship with the Beagles represented something very precious to him. He had good reason to keep it alive. 'If you count every little thing,' he says, 'and that on one day I might compete in five events, on average, I'd say, I compete between seventy and ninety times a year. I like it.

'It gets away from all the rubbish about being a star. It's getting out there and meeting guys who train three, four, five, six times a week. They do it for the same reason I do it. They do it not because they're getting paid but because they enjoy running. They enjoy getting out and meeting the boys, having a good laugh.

'My track work isn't like that any more. It's more serious. It's such bloody hard work all the time with everybody taking it so seriously. You wouldn't think it was fun. Christ, you go to an international and nobody wants to talk to you for fear of losing energy.'

The longer I was there and the more time we spent together, the clearer it became that that period wasn't quite as wonderful and carefree as I had originally thought. The change that I first perceived as maturity was actually more complicated. There was a growing awareness of the outside world.

Most evident was his difficulty with the attention he received. In 1979 he was a rising star, a new face that occasionally appeared in the newspapers in connection with an exotic event nobody really understood. By 1981 he had become a personality. In the press, news of his activities had moved from the sports section to the society page. His being spotted playing tennis with a woman was reason enough for gossip. That Thompson was a confirmed stay-at-home who had been seeing the same woman faithfully for years was less interesting. His gregarious manner, and the number of his friends who happen to be women, were enough to keep the rumour mills grinding. He was, after all, a public person, and an attractive black man in a white society. Reason enough, apparently, for a great deal of speculation, and more attention than he was comfortable with.

As a result, he rarely went anywhere he did not have to, especially to town, to somewhere as public as a department store. That rising murmur of recognition in a crowd that once gave him pleasure had become a source of agitation. More than once, while standing in line at McDonald's, fully planning to collect his hamburger, fries and coke, take them to a booth and eat like a normal person, he would be routed by the aggressive adoration of other customers, and another meal would be eaten in the front seat of his car.

'1979 was a long time ago,' says Thompson. 'I don't know if I enjoy the attention any less now, but I'm less tolerant of it. I'm not into being other people's property. Things have been changing all along, in fact since 1978. People always assume that part of you is theirs, and you're there because of them. They're always coming up to me, when I'm training, when I'm eating, and they expect me to be really friendly about it. It's not the kind of thing I would do.

'It seems my world has shrunk. There are fewer places I can go and be comfortable and not harassed. But I quite like it at home. I enjoy my house. And cinemas are dark.'

More serious was the problem of training. Ever since he returned to London from Farney Close, Thompson had had strict and reliable guidance in his career. From that afternoon at Crystal Palace in 1974 when he first met Bob Mortimer, through the six-year relationship with Bruce Longden, there had always been someone there with an answer. It may not always have been the best answer, but it relieved him of the responsibility of making the decision. Then, it didn't matter if he budgeted his time not quite perfectly, or his technique was less than it could be. He had enough youth, time, talent and an incredible amount of energy to compensate.

161

Suddenly, by 1981, the situation had changed. While he respected Krzesinski and liked working with him, he wasn't completely comfortable with the programme the coach had laid out for him. He was, for example, unhappy without a morning training session. He had always worked in the morning and liked to feel he was making full use of his day. He was also concerned about getting the right quality of instruction in some of his skill events, especially discus and shot.

'It's the most difficult period I've ever faced,' says Thompson of the time. 'I'm threequarters of the way there, and I've got nobody to take me the rest. I know all the basics of what I need to know, and it's just a question of putting some of the finer points together. I can't find the right people at the right places at the right time to help me. And even when I can get to them, they all have something different to say. Everybody's got so much advice, it's difficult to know who's right and who's not.'

Then there was the ruckus over the European Combined Events Cup, scheduled for Birmingham the last weekend in August. It was the intention of the British athletics authorities to show off their new sports facility in the Midlands, and their newly crowned Olympic decathlon champion. Unfortunately, things failed to work out smoothly for anyone.

According to Thompson, the trouble began towards the end of 1980, not long after the Games ended. The autumn is the normal time for making financial arrangements for the coming year. By 1980 Thompson was receiving about £4000 in annual support from the Sports Aid Foundation, sent out in monthly cheques. Additional money was available for training expenses. While the Foundation is supposed to be an independent body, raising money for athletes without intervention or assistance, it works closely with the British Amateur Athletic Board. The board of governors of the Foundation may be advised by various sports authorities as to who deserves to receive grants, but it is the BAAB which guides its policy decisions.

'In the past they'd always given me money to live on, and I'd always performed to the best of my ability,' says Thompson. 'But that year they saw fit to tell me where I had to compete. They said if I didn't compete in Birmingham, they wouldn't give me any money. I said OK then, that's it.'

All this was communicated in a series of letters, beginning in October 1980. As usual, Thompson sent the Foundation a statement of his aims for the coming year. He wanted, he said, to recapture his world record in the decathlon. There were three opportunities to accomplish this: the annual decathlon championships in Götzis, a dual meet between Canada and Great Britain in Saskatchewan, and the European Cup in Birmingham.

The Foundation responded that unless he could guarantee his presence in Birmingham in August, he would get no money. Thompson wrote back that he could 'never guarantee' his competing anywhere, since that always depended on his physical condition. The Foundation was not satisfied.

Though no public statement had been released by the Sports Aid Foundation, its own financial problems caused a definite change in policy for 1981. Because less money was available, and because there were more athletes getting financial assistance, the Foundation imposed new limitations on the money it gave out.

While all this was going on, the secretary of the British Amateur Athletic Board was David Shaw. He, as much as any single individual, was involved with the controversy over the European Cup. 'In 1981 they [the Foundation] categorically stated that grants would only be given as preparation for world, European or equivalent events,' said Shaw about the matter. 'From our point of view, that was defined as the European Cup. If athletes were not going for the European Cup, they couldn't be put into the pot for grants.

'In the case of Daley's application, where he indicated

163

that all he wanted to do in 1981 was to go for a world record, we indicated to the Sports Aid Foundation that if we were all playing the same game, it would have to be the European Cup. When that was put back to Daley, he just let the whole thing drop.'

So, in effect, did the Foundation, because at that point – October 1980 – all financial assistance to Daley Thompson stopped. He went on training as usual for his season, but it was to be a season without Birmingham.

As far as he was concerned, the matter was closed. The BAAB, however, continued to promote the European Cup as if the nation's top multi-events athlete would be its star. The event was heavily sponsored, and to be covered by the BBC, mostly because of Thompson's presence. But there was no further communication between Board and athlete until a month before the event was to take place. In the meantime, the Board, which controls the participation of British athletes in international events, refused to permit Thompson to compete in Götzis. His one remaining competition of the year, as part of the British team in Canada, was washed out by a second day downpour with him on world-record pace.

'Four weeks before Birmingham they came and asked me to compete,' says Thompson, adding that four weeks is too little time to prepare for a decathlon if he were not already doing so. 'I told them we'd already settled that. They said they didn't remember. Can you believe that?'

It was about a week before the competition when the news began to appear in the London papers: 'Britain Waiting for Thompson', was the headline that ran the weekend before the semifinals in Brussels; the day before the team was announced, 'Thompson Uncertain'.

Four days before the meeting began, after the list of participating athletes appeared without Thompson's name, John Rodda, athletics correspondent for the *Guardian* and also, incidentally, president of the Essex Beagles and, till then, an ardent Daley supporter, wrote

164

scathingly under the headline 'Thompson Quits Decathlon Cup'. From the *Guardian*:

Daley Thompson, the Olympic decathlon champion, is in
danger of losing his Sports Aid Foundation grant and more
friends as a result of declining the invitation to compete for
Britain in the European Combined Events Cup at
Birmingham this weekend, the most important decathlon
competition of the summer. He is also in danger of becoming
'Daley who?'

If the column had not given the impression early on
that Thompson had taken grant money in poor faith, it
clarified its position in the ninth paragraph: 'The Sports
Aid Foundation grant was made specifically, I understand, to help his preparation for the European Cup and
unless there is some satisfactory explanation as to why
he is not taking part then it could be withdrawn.' There
was other criticism of Thompson's actions, and sugges-
tions that he wanted more money from the Foundation
and had used the European Cup as leverage.

David Shaw left the BAAB late in 1981, and in
December became general secretary of the Independent
Television Companies Association Limited, the organization that brings those companies together for such
matters as overall policy, programming and advertising.

'I think that where this all went adrift is that people
like myself, associated closely with the sport,' Shaw said,
'couldn't believe that at the end of the day Thompson
wouldn't do it. And I think we found too late that
he wasn't going to do it. We were left frustrated and
embarrassed. A little better communication, a little more
careful handling, might have avoided the whole thing.'

He admits that withholding grant money was not
the only punitive action taken because of Thompson's
position on the European Cup. His refusal to go to
Birmingham also cost him permission to compete in
Götzis, according to Shaw, 'more or less as punishment.
He tested us on this particular point at a time when
that was a very important point to stand on. It's very

165

important that the British Board keep control of the sport at that level, and part of keeping control is to say to people who put a lot of money into the sport, "Yes, this is the big one and we'll get the top team out." It was the wrong time for a top athlete to exert that particular independence.'

Had Shaw and the Board known Thompson better, they might have approached the situation differently. One of the few ways of guaranteeing Daley Thompson will not show up at a particular place at a particular time is to demand his presence.

'For everything that I've ever learned,' Thompson said earlier, 'the overriding lesson is that I have to be in control of everything, and not be told to be here, to be there.'

As embarrassing as it was for the British athletics establishment, the episode was more costly for Thompson. It cost him financially; he was refused money from the Foundation from October 1980 to 1981 and, because of that incident, he has not applied for a grant since. It cost him publicly; he was presented to the British people as money-grabbing and unpatriotic. Most important to Thompson, it cost him as an athlete who loves competition. It was inconceivable that he should miss a decathlon at Birmingham attended not only by the best decathletes in the world – including his old rival, Kratschmer – but his own friends. Greg Richards was there competing, as was Pan Zeniou.

'I'm bound to have been there, aren't I,' he says. 'I'm a decathlete – I do decathlons. And this would have been good fun. Everyone who was anybody was there. If they hadn't gone about it that way, I'd have been there, too.'

In response to the charges of his being unpatriotic, Thompson says, 'Patriotism has nothing to do with it. The issues are competition, and a man's pride.'

There were other factors complicating Thompson's life towards the end of 1981, factors that made those relatively carefree days of two years before seem much more distant. Though he was only twenty-three years old, he was beginning to suffer the sense of time passing. Not so much for himself. He had worked so hard to develop his control over the world around him that he had even managed to stop time, or at least to slow the effects of its erosion.

'The work gets harder every year,' he said. 'But that's the plan. The training takes more out of me each year because I try and do more each year. I'm basically fitter, which lets me do more and yet end up feeling only as bad as the year before. So while it never gets easier, I never lose ground either.'

Those around him were not so successful. Steve Green, the fine sprinter, decided after 1979 to commit himself full-time to his studies. Dave Baptiste, having suffered through a series of injuries and rising and falling dedication to his running, took whatever training he wanted at Mayesbrook Park, near where he lived. Snowy Brooks, approaching forty, was holding down two jobs and managed to work out only at weekends. The old group, for one reason or another, was fading away.

'It doesn't go all of a sudden,' says Thompson. 'It goes from seven to five days, to four days to three days, over a year or two years. You don't notice it to start with, until it's too late. Then you mention it a bit. You realize they found other things, or they realized it's never to be.'

The 'it' that is to be or not to be in athletics is a highly individual goal. It is what each athlete wants out of his or her sport. For a Daley Thompson it is greatness, to be the best decathlete who ever lived. For a Dave Baptiste it is a place on the British team going to the European Championships or the Commonwealth Games. For most, the time and resources going into fulfilling that dream are limited to their early years and, as the youth of their teens is replaced by the adulthood of their twenties, the commitment weakens and eventually they give up. Thompson, the most committed of all, the one whose resources in pursuit of the dream seem

167

limitless, will certainly last the longest. Which means that, at some point, he pursues it alone.

'I won't be alone for long,' he says. 'I've got Zeni's promise that he'll stick it out till 1984. I know he'll do that. Maybe I can even talk him into two more years, you never know. I'm only going on till 1988. Two, four years – that's not so bad. I did the first four years by myself. And there's always Greg. And when Greg goes, I'll get Slaney to lose 150 pounds and become a decathlete.'

Though joking, Thompson was not smiling. The drama is a variation on a theme played out in sport of all kinds. Not the classic about the athlete getting old and facing his own mortality, struggling to fulfil the potential he saw in himself as a young man. It is the one about the star who, by virtue of his superior ability and commitment, survives to see those with whom he has trained and competed slowly pass from the scene.

In team sports there is a structure provided. The old pro is the man around whom management builds its team of the future. Lesser athletes are replaced from year to year with an endless supply of new, young talent, with the knowledge that this old pro will provide the stability so necessary to make the team win. He is the conduit from the glories of yesterday to what management hopes will be the glories of tomorrow.

It is more personal in track and field. There is no firm organization, no squad of players, with every position to be filled by some vast, unseen mechanism. The people involved are individuals, friends mostly, many of whom have grown up together, and they see in their daily lives a commonality of need, of desire. Such groups of athletes share the strongest of bonds, the closest of friendships. Each is there every day by virtue of his own energy. They all understand why they are there and what they get from the experience. But they do not share the same talent, and they don't share the same goals. That makes for real conflicts within those very special friendships.

In this particular group, the man closest to Daley

Thompson has always been Pan Zeniou, the man Daley calls 'the Greek'. It had been Zeniou's dream to be a world-class decathlete, but he never had the benefit of good coaching during his crucial early years and when he was eighteen he injured his knee, which restricted his jumping thereafter. He has reached a balance within himself, as do so many athletes, working not for glory but for some inner satisfaction.

Very early in their relationship, a symbiotic pattern developed between the two men. 'We've been to a lot of meetings together,' says Zeniou. 'I was in Spain with him in 1977 when he broke the world junior record. After each event he would come to me for a little chat, and he would go away more inspired, on more of a high. I didn't say anything really. That's just the way it has always been. He comes to me and talks, and he feels better. And when he feels better, I feel better.'

The presence of Zeniou at meetings has been important to Thompson since the very beginning. Converting that circus atmosphere into just another day's training is an ability Zeniou has, and Thompson relies on it. He even suggests that had Zeniou been in Prague with him for the European Championships in 1978, the outcome would have been different. 'Yep,' he says, 'if Zeni had been there, I'd have won.'

There was never serious competition between the two. Thompson proved himself to be the superior athlete in his very first year in the decathlon. His total the day of the Olympic trials in 1976 was higher than Zeniou has ever scored. Possibly only in an event like the decathlon could such a situation exist without continued tension. Both athletes working together, striving to improve, but at their own level. Still, it takes maturity to embrace that philosophy.

Pan Zeniou, on perspective: 'Early on with Daley, it was a problem. We both put in the same work and we got different results. I understood that. The guy's talented. He may be the greatest athlete in the world today. I never saw myself as that. But it was hard then.

169

I don't feel that frustration any more. He's that much better, and I can see that. We have different goals. He wants to put the world record out of sight; I just want to be able to feel that all the work, the sacrifices throughout the years, have been worthwhile.'

The relationship, now entering its eighth year, resembles a marriage. The two men train together every day, until sometimes eight or nine at night. On those rare occasions when one of them doesn't want to train, the other will goad him into it. While they normally meet at Haringey or Crystal Palace, should one of them have trouble with his car, the other is there to pick him up, though they live on opposite sides of London. One morning after a snowstorm, when Zeniou couldn't get off work, Thompson drove to his job at lunchtime so the two of them could head for nearby Parliament Hill and run their drills on the uncleared track.

That friendship does not stop with training. Few of Thompson's personal plans do not include Zeniou. Patricia Quinlan – whom Daley calls Tisha, or Fish – accepts this as a normal part of their relationship, along with working weekends and Daley's training months in San Diego. She has learned by now to expect it, and wasn't at all surprised that, when she and Daley returned from their vacation in Mauritius after the Olympics, he went on another vacation with 'the boys'.

Thompson, because of his status, gets invited to a variety of sub-decathlon competitions, mostly sponsored by private promotors or universities, and he does his best to get Zeniou invited as well. Sometimes he flatly refuses otherwise.

'I've been really lucky,' says Zeniou. 'Athletics has given me so many things: good friends, a lot of pleasure, good memories, and I've travelled around the world.'

But within the next fourteen months he would be thirty, a crisis age for any athlete, but especially difficult for one who feels he has not met his potential. For the past two years, Zeniou has been haunted by his situation with his sport. 'Every year the enthusiasm gets lower and lower and lower,' he said in that winter of 1981. 'I've tried very hard. All right, a lot of it was wrong in the beginning, but I've put the energy in, and I haven't justified my training. I haven't got the scores I think I'm capable of. [His best score, 7558 points, came in the European Cup at Birmingham that summer.]

'As I get older I begin to think more in terms of material goods. It's important for me to get a new car, for example, and I can't. I still live with my folks – I'd like to get a flat. I've tried to explain this to Daley and Richard, and they don't seem to understand. They think I'm being too materialistic. But you get to a certain age and you need things; you need to make some kind of life for yourself outside athletics. I've given athletics a good shot. I've been involved with the decathlon for more than ten years, training seriously for seven.'

At that point, late in December, he was making plans to go to San Diego with Thompson in January. He had arranged a three-month leave from his job. To help cover expenses, he was selling his car, a beaten up yellow estate with one door from the junk yard and a rearview mirror that sat casually on the dash, unattached. That winter was the coldest, most snowy in London for a century, and he was looking forward to training in the warm sunshine.

'I have a lot I want to work on in San Diego,' he said. 'I want to get there and get to it, because I really feel I can accomplish something. Then I look at this coming season and I say to myself, I want to score 8000 points. If I do, yes, I'll be happy. I'll be over the moon. But it would be different if I'd done that three years ago. For a man of thirty to be scoring that, it's nothing.'

He was talking inside the gymnasium at Haringey, off in the corner where the vault pads are stored when not in use. All around him athletes were working out, training. Not for the Olympics, and most of them not for any competition so major as an international, but simply for their own satisfaction. The difference with

171

Pan Zeniou was that he was caught in the space between their world and that of Daley Thompson.

'Don't get me wrong,' he said. 'We have a relationship that gives a lot to both of us. It gives me pleasure when he does well, especially when he does something special, like breaking the world record. And I know he gets pleasure out of my improvement. We both work hard, for each other really. He works to help me, and I work to help him. Part of his record is my doing; I like to think that.'

His voice trailed off, and he just sat there for a few minutes, listening to the sound of weights clanging against rubber mats. 'He wants me to go on to 1984,' he said. 'I don't know if I can do it. It will be very difficult for me. Financially, it will be very difficult. I want to – I want to be part of it – but it will be difficult. If I go on to 1984 with him, I'll be thirty-one. What have I got at the end?'

The importance of one athlete to another is as often misunderstood by the outside world as is the attraction of an athlete to his sport. In both cases, the relationship is highly personal. Daley Thompson on Pan Zeniou: 'Zeni expects a lot of me. He's always there, ready to give me some kind of verbal or physical abuse if the need arises. If I don't feel so good, Zeni's always trying to bolster me and make me feel better.

'After the record, I felt really tired. I told Bruce that I'd lost it all, and he wasn't being any help to me. He wasn't saying anything; if I didn't want to train it was OK. And it's not OK. I needed somebody to say it's not OK. I needed somebody to say, "Come on down and go to work," or "Come down and see the boys." Zeni did that.

'And with training now, he's really important. We both have our ideas of how we should look at whatever we do. A perfect model for the discus has to be 6 feet 7 inches and have 25-foot arms and weigh 350 pounds. Me and Zeni are 6 feet 1 inch, with short arms and no legs. But we've been doing it long enough that we know

172

what we should look like, and what works here and what works there. We've talked this over a lot, and we both know what we want. He knows what I want to look like and I know what he wants to look like.'

The slow drifting apart of his group was disturbing to Thompson not only because he missed their company during training, but because they were his family, an integral part of his life. They were the people to whom he was closest, the people who had known him longest and understood him best. But their primary bond was training. Once that bond was broken, it would have been easy for the family to dissolve. Thompson fought to keep that from happening. No social gathering was complete without each and every one of the old gang. That Christmas the Rayment–Thompson house was jammed. Nobody knows for sure how many friends came by that weekend, but I personally helped wrap nearly thirty presents the week before. And for Tisha's birthday, Thompson took Tisha, Doreen, Tisha's friend Pam, Zeni, Greg and Jackie Jackson to see the Pointer Sisters at the Dominion Theatre.

Thompson was even able to pull some of the dropouts back in for an occasional training session. Saturdays usually, early in the morning at Battersea Park. As many of the group as he could persuade: Zeni, Snowy, Greg, even Baptiste when he could manage it, Thompson coaxing him over the phone, convincing him to come in by train. I was there for one of those sessions, the first time in a long while that Daley had talked Dave into coming out.

It was early in December. While the first of the winter's snowfalls wouldn't arrive until the following week, it was still pretty cold. They started drifting in shortly after 9 a.m. First Daley, then Zeni and Greg. Brooks had picked up Baptiste at the station, and they arrived last. For the first ten minutes there were lots of jokes about the insanity of being out there on that cold, bleak morning. They had that section of the park practically to themselves: one couple was on the tennis courts and a few people were walking dogs. The track was completely theirs.

They began with a brisk jog around the park to warm up, followed by half a dozen sprints, some 300-metre runs and a series of charges up the surrounding hills. The banter among four of them – Greg Richards is a very quiet man – was rapid and continual, with Baptiste receiving an extra measure of abuse because he wasn't quite keeping up. Brooks also looked a little slow, but nobody messed with him because everybody knew callisthenics were coming up. Brooks, as always, ran the callisthenics sessions.

The whole thing took about ninety minutes, but they were ninety very active minutes, and by the time they plopped down in the infield of the track, warming themselves in what there was of the sunshine, it was as if war buddies had been reunited, brought together from different parts of the world. They joked about 'the old days', when they really used to work hard, and each man brought up his favourite training story. Dave Baptiste was last.

'The worst of all of us was Green,' he said, referring to Steve Green. 'He wanted me to work out with him on 25 December. I said, "But Steve, it's Christmas Day." He said, "All right, we'll only train in the morning. I know a place that's open." Sure enough, he meets me on the other side of Blackwall Tunnel and takes me to a track. It's totally deserted, freezing cold, and some chap's collecting admission.'

They all got together on other Saturdays, and Thompson enjoyed it. It was like the old days, and there were things about those days that he missed. Certainly it was a simpler time, less complicated by financial, career and training decisions; and while one would not assume that a man of twenty-three would be mourning the loss of his youth, every defection from such an intimate group saddens those who remain, pointing out the tenuousness of their situation.

At that particular time it seemed no front was secure.

174

Not only were his training friends disappearing in 1981; rivals too were vanishing. There were new Russians to replace Alexandr Grebenyuk, who had beaten him in the European Championships in Prague. All the Americans he knew were gone. There were even young, talented West Germans on the scene. After six years, Jürgen Hingsen had supplanted Thompson's old friend Kratschmer as their number one. There was special poignancy in that.

On the last weekend in November, at the generous invitation of Adidas, Thompson went to Bremen, Germany, to take part in *Sport Speil Spannung*, an evening of athletics and entertainment at the city hall, a huge auditorium right in the middle of town. Daley knew only that he would be playing some 'athletic games' with Kratschmer.

All afternoon before the Saturday night festivities, reporters and fans from across Germany kept ringing Thompson's room, wanting interviews, autographs and for him to pose for pictures. Many asked what he thought of the 'big competition', to which he always made some joking reply. But all the excitement was making him uncomfortable and he didn't think any of it was funny. Even when the competition is a game, Thompson doesn't like to lose.

'I've got a feeling somebody we both know has been training six months for this,' he said to me on the way to the auditorium, 'and somebody else we know is going to get duffed up.'

It ended up being an evening of genuine fun, twenty-one separate acts including gymnastics, precision dancing, exhibitions of American football, soccer and frisbee, and something called Olympia-Revanche, which featured Daley and Guido competing in several very strange events: a long jump in flippers, a race on bicycles with off-centred wheels, an obstacle course on wheel-equipped skis, and other similar kinds of madness.

All through that long evening, waiting for the programme to begin, watching the acts, and later in the

175

huge room where sandwiches and drinks were served, the two men sat and talked. They joked with each other about still being in off-season shape. (Guido confessed to weighing 96 kilogrammes, and Daley insisted he looked closer to 100; Kratschmer smiled impishly and shrugged.) They talked about decathlons past and future, spending most of their time on the coming games of the following summer in Greece. And through it all, much of it interrupted by people asking for autographs, asking them to pose together for a snapshot, there was a clearly visible warmth, a genuine mutual affection and respect between the two, rivals at one level or another since 1976.

After the programme – it went on till well past midnight – we all sat and talked together while sandwiches, soft drinks and huge glasses of beer were passed around a room full of long tables. It was the first opportunity I'd had to talk to Kratschmer since two years before, in Mainz. We talked of the Olympics, and his plan to retire afterwards.

'Moscow,' he said, and shook his head. 'When you work for so long, for a goal, and it . . .' He stopped, gesturing with his hands, motioning in circles, suggesting nothingness. 'You have no . . .' Again he stopped, and said something in German to the man next to him, who responded first in German, and then in English. Kratschmer continued. 'Completion,' he said. 'And you must have completion.' I asked if the world record was not enough, and he nodded. 'It's important,' he said, 'but not enough. It's not the Olympics. It's not the gold medal.'

He was then twenty-eight years old and did appear a little heavy, even for that time of year. He had completed work towards his physical education degree at Mainz. In another year he would have his degree in biology and could teach. If he wanted that. I asked if he did. An expression came over his face I could not read and there were no words to help me. I asked how long he would continue to compete. 'I don't know,' he said. 'It's not simple now. As long as I can, I think.'

Though Thompson did not discuss Kratschmer at any length after the trip to Bremen, I could tell it was difficult seeing him like that, even painful. Guido was not only a man he liked, but someone with whom he could identify. Probably one of the few in the whole world. He could empathize with someone who had worked towards a goal and was now having the right to compete for that goal taken away. To deny the culmination of years of labour is to question one's very existence.

Seeing Kratschmer was evidence of a hard reality, and Thompson seemed to understand that all too well. That, perhaps, was the change I sensed in him that winter. The outside world had begun to intrude more into his life, and he had hardened in response. He had learned how that world could be – capricious, unyielding, dogmatic – and he was not about to bend to any force like that. It reminded me of stories I had heard about him when, in 1975, he first became serious about his athletics. To aid that commitment he generated a new degree of intensity – 'nastiness' Bob Mortimer called it – about his pursuit of his sport. What I seemed to be seeing was an extreme sensitivity to anything that might sap one ounce of vital strength, take one moment of valuable time. However antisocial he might occasionally appear, he did not care. He was a man obsessed.

If this were the case, it explained many things about the man and the athlete I encountered. His resolve, if possible, was greater than two years earlier. No longer was it a matter of not considering defeat; losing now loomed as an enemy rivalled only by death. He had restructured his thinking since Prague. In 1978 he did not think defeat was possible. By 1981 he had accepted it was possible in a dozen different ways, and had systematically gone about combating those ways. He would accept nothing but victory, would countenance no excuse. No extenuating circumstances were admissible in his court. Not injury, not an act of God, not anything.

'People don't need to know about injuries,' he

177

responded to a question about his not discussing them. 'They're just excuses. You're always reading about athletes saying they're injured, and the next week they'll do something really well and people will say how marvellous that they could do it with such an injury. Well, I'm not into that stuff.

'If I get out there to perform I expect to perform well. If the injury's that bad, I'm not going to do it; if it's not that bad, then I'm going to perform well. That's the way it is. I either do it to the best of my ability or I don't do it at all.' And if the wind's blowing up a gale, or if it's raining? 'There's nothing I can do about the rain. If it's raining, it's just another obstacle to overcome, and if I'm going to vault well then I'm going to overcome that rain better than the other guys.

'The whole thing is a competition; you have to be able to overcome anything that comes up. To be able to prepare yourself – that's what it's all about. To prepare yourself to have two false starts in the 100, then have the best start of your life on the third one when you're not meant to; to be able to come up with the best shot of your life after two fouls and, after a hard day, run the fastest 400 of your life.

'That's what it's all about. And if it's raining and nobody's feeling good, and you've just seen two guys foul out before you and you're on your third attempt, then you clear by miles and make a pb.'

He had completed the process begun so very long ago, probably on the dirt track at Farney Close School. He had, at least in his own mind, taken complete control of his life, and accepted full responsibility for everything he did. That applies regardless of the cost. He had proved just how far he would pursue his control in the situation with the Athletic Board over Birmingham. He didn't want to miss that decathlon, but he felt he had to make it clear that he was nobody's man but his own, no matter how much it hurt. ('It's not easy, cutting off your nose to spite your face,' he said in reference to the incident.)

178

He had worked hard to lay the perfect foundation for the next stage of his athletics career. Physically, emotionally, politically, he was ready. 'The first kind of pressure is over, the proving it,' he's said of the early years. 'I've done it. I've proved what I set out to do. I broke the world record, I won the gold medal in the Olympics.

'Now it's the search for perfection. I haven't spent the last eight years doing this so that I can win just one gold medal and break one world record. I'm in it for more than that. Two golds, three gold medals. Pushing the record so high, it'll stand for years. As for 9000 points – it's just the next stop in a natural progression. I plan on taking that step as soon as I can.'

There are many who believe such goals are too ambitious in this age of super athletes and super commitments. One sceptic is Bob Mathias, the American, who was the only man younger than Thompson to compete in an Olympic decathlon: younger by a few months. He's also the only man ever to win two Olympic gold medals in the decathlon; his first in London in 1948 when he was seventeen, his second four years later in Helsinki.

'Things are so different now in athletics,' says Mathias. 'I think two golds is a record that will stand for ever.' Mathias speaks with some authority about the world of track and field. Since June 1977 he has been head of the Olympic Training Center in Colorado Springs, Colorado, about seventy-five miles south of Denver. The centre, converted from an abandoned military installation, Ent Air Force Base, gave America its first permanent training site, where Olympic athletes could live and train free.

'I think I heard about the decathlon three or four months before I started working for it,' he says. 'I worked out for about three months, tried my hand at a couple of competitions, and then I went to England and won the thing. Even for the next Olympics, I didn't train like they do today.'

179

Mathias, strong and handsome at fifty-two, was one of the earliest athletes to make commercial profit from his Olympic success. Not only did he appear in ads for hair tonic, trousers, shaving cream and vitamins after his second victory; he made four films and starred in his own television series. Later he served four terms as a US congressman from California, and ran a successful boys' camp. And through it all he has kept up with the decathlon, and has known all the decathletes who have represented the USA since he competed. While he has been at Colorado Springs, he has made a point of meeting each new group to talk about training and competition and the changes in the event.

'They train so much longer and harder than I ever did,' he says. 'Every day, week after week, year after year. And once you've done that for four or five years, it's awfully hard to go back and do it again. That's why I don't think you're ever going to get a guy to win twice again. Not anybody. It's just too tough. The competition is too tough; the work is too tough. I don't think they can do it any more.'

Thompson just smiles when he hears this. It is, to him, one more challenge, one more 'something to overcome', like the rain or a pulled hamstring. 'He doesn't remember,' he says. 'You get all involved with it, and it just goes on and on. It has its own life. It takes over.'

On one of the last days I was in London, just before Christmas, when there was snow on the ground and the night before had been bitterly cold, come morning, Daley's car refused to start. He had called Zeniou to tell him he wouldn't make it for training that day, and his friend insisted on coming over to pick him up. They would go over to Crystal Palace, he said, which was closer than Haringey. We were sitting in the kitchen, drinking coffee, talking about life with the decathlon, what it was really like.

'Apart from Zeni, who has a threequarter understanding,' he said, 'nobody really understands. Even people who try. Even you. You have a little bit of understand-

180

ing, but you only know it from the outside. You know what it's about, but you don't know the inside.

'Even people who do other sports seriously, they don't understand. It's that different from what they do. And there's no way I can explain it to someone who only does sport for recreation. He's got nothing to relate it to. He's so far back it's like trying to see details on the moon with your naked eye.

'It's not like going to work. It's not getting up in the morning, going to work and coming home in the evening. It's a whole lifestyle. It's everything. Everything is involved in getting up and doing it. It's more like being a monk. Not because you abstain or anything, but just because there is nothing else. You wake up in the morning – you don't start praying, but you start reading journals – and the whole day follows in line. It's all directed toward one thing.'

He looked into his cup as if some message were contained here. 'People are always asking me what happens when it's all over. If this is so important, they say, what happens when it's gone. I know I'm going to have a family. I want to be a good father.' He thought for a moment, then went on. 'I'll miss the excitement of a big competition. Nothing will ever be able to replace that. No matter what I do, I'll never reach the same kinds of highs, or the same kinds of lows. I won't try to replace it – I'll just do something else. I don't know what it will be, but whatever it is, it will be a total commitment.

'But I'll go on competing till I can't any more. They have seniors' events, you know, and old men's scoring tables. I'm going to get into some of that. Competition is what I am – I do love it. Winning is a great part of it, but just being there . . .' His voice trailed off. Slowly he started to smile.

'Yea, competition, I'll still be there. I can see it years from now, me and Zeni, competing in wheelchairs, being pushed. I'll never stop competing. It's me. More than anything, it's me, all over.'

Coda

It is a pleasant spring afternoon in 1982. The place is Choc Sportsman Stadium, track and field facility of San Diego State University. The time of year is not really important here, which is one of the fine things about this section of southern California. The weather is almost always the same – perfect. That makes the seasons seem to run together, as do the years. The bright sunshine, the clear blue skies, the moderate temperatures. They are here all the time.

For Daley Thompson, this is his fourth season in San Diego. Each winter since 1979 he has left the wet cold of London and flown into the sunshine and warmth, to run and jump and throw, to ready himself for the challenges that begin in May and continue through the late summer, in places with faraway names, Götzis and Prague, Moscow and Athens and Brisbane.

He always brings a little of his home with him. He comes with his reading material, his journals, his scoring tables and his book of metric conversion, and his tape player with a dozen or more cassettes, Wilton Felder and John Klemmer and, of course, George Benson. He also brings company. In the beginning he came with his coach, Bruce Longden, then with Snowy Brooks. More recently, it's Pan Zeñiou. Once here, there is always Richard Slaney, the giant from Crawley. Much as he likes all that San Diego has to offer, he likes a bit of England as well.

It is mid-afternoon, and the track complex is nearly deserted. Most of the students are still on their spring break, that annual holiday loosely scheduled round Easter. Only a few are here to work out for the coming meeting, the Bruce Jenner Classic a week away in San Jose, some 550 miles to the north. A couple of young women are working inside the discus cage, a high horse-shoe of chainlink fence protecting a polyurethane circle. The surface of the circle – like the other throwing areas and the long jump and vault runways, and the 400-metre track that encircles it all – is dried hard from the sun, and has taken on the cracked, faded look of old, red clay. Around that hard track, four men jog at a slow pace.

Zeniou and Slaney sit on the infield grass and watch Thompson as he stretches. He uses one of the barriers on the steeple-chase course for balance, holding on as he spreads his legs wide apart and stretches, timing himself with the digital stopwatch he wears on his wrist.

The other two have completed their stretching. They came straight here while Thompson stopped first at the house of Joe Briski – former San Diego State student and assistant track coach, and still holder of the university's record for the longest hammer throw, 195 feet 2 inches. Since his effort to recruit Thompson in 1978, the men have been friends. Thompson has rented an apartment for himself, Slaney and Zeniou just a block from Briski's house, and is over there regularly, to collect mail, watch television and socialize.

He works very patiently on his stretching, not something he's always done. When he was sixteen he was told by Bob Mortimer how important it is to stretch every day, but he dismissed the notion. He now regrets that youthful arrogance, and stretches before workouts, and again at night before bed.

When Thompson has finished, the three men head over to the long-jump area. They make a strange sight: on their own, the two decathletes are formidable figures, but beside Slaney they are children, and underdeveloped at that. As they walk the joking begins, cracks about the weight Slaney put on over the winter and has yet to lose,

183

accusations about who ate the last of Thompson's sugar-coated breakfast cereal, unrealistically low estimates of how many points Zeniou will score at the Mt SAC Relays coming up in two weeks outside Los Angeles, their last stop before going home.

The flexibility in this schedule, the jocular byplay, the availability of facilities – they're all part of the attraction of San Diego. There is nothing to separate Thompson from his work here. He gets up early and reads, comes out for breakfast at about nine o'clock, and is at the track by 10.30. He breaks for lunch with the boys about 1.30, rests and is back at the track by three where he stays till six or so. Then he has dinner, watches television at Briski's and goes home to bed. It is, for him, ideal.

'You can do anything you like out there,' he once said, describing San Diego. 'You can take the day off and train all night. You can get up early in the morning and train, or you can sleep in the morning and train all afternoon and evening. You can do anything. The track's always there, and nobody's ever on it.

'And there's nobody there to make any demands on my time, ever. Just me, the track, Slaney and big Zeni.' It is this last which is so alluring; just as important as the good weather and fine facilities, which are only ten minutes' drive from his apartment. There are no public appearances, no command performances for press or officials of any kind. There is no personal pressure, not even the subtle obligation to eat when he's not hungry because someone has prepared food and he doesn't want to offend.

Nobody and nothing but training. That's how he likes it and it seems to agree with him. Never have I seen him in better shape. He seems bigger than when I saw him last, at the indoor pentathlon in Toronto at the end of January. He cannot be much bigger – a pound or so, which would not show on his frame – but he seems bigger, more muscular.

If scores are an indication, a little California serves him well. He stopped in Toronto on the way over from

London, before beginning the more serious stage of technical training reserved for San Diego. While he won the meeting, scoring 4100 points in the 55-metre hurdles, shot, long jump, high jump and 1000-metre run – one of some 30,240 combinations taken from the decathlon and often used in minor, multi-event meetings – he was not overwhelming. He defeated Dave Steen, the Canadian decathlon champion, by 87 points. Then, after less than a month's work in the California sunshine, he journeyed to Texas and scored 4315 in a similar competition. His closest competitors – Steen among them – scored 4066, 4044 and 4032.

That was nearly two months ago. Now he is clearly ready for the most challenging season of his career: Götzis, the last weekend in May; the European Championships in Athens early in September; the Commonwealth Games in Brisbane the first week of October.

The banter among the three continues. As they approach the long-jump pit Slaney says something about Zeniou's not being able to put the shot farther than 40 feet, 8 feet below his best. Zeni responds by turning his back, then dropping and replacing his running shorts.

'Bet you wouldn't long jump like that!' says Slaney.

'How much?' demands Zeniou.

'Twenty dollars.'

Zeniou looks at Slaney, and then over to Thompson.

'I'll cover that,' smiles Daley.

'You're on,' says Zeniou, who looks quickly around the track. The girls are busy with their discus, and the joggers are just passing. He waits till their backs are to him, then pulls off his shorts. He starts to lay them down but, glancing at his friends, thinks better of such folly. Folding the shorts neatly into his left hand, he rocks once, twice on the runway, then shoots down the faded red course, hitting the take-off board and flying into the air.

As he hits the board, Slaney and Thompson let out a whoop and start applauding. The girls in the discus cage turn, see the soaring Greek, look a second time to verify

185

that is in fact what they are seeing as he lands and, flushed with embarrassment, turn quickly away.

Thompson and Slaney fall to the ground in hysterics as Zeniou replaces his shorts, bows, then reminds them there is still work to be done. Slowly they get to it. After a time with the long jump, Slaney watching to see that they don't go over the line, Thompson and Zeniou jumping, the huge discus thrower goes over to work on his own event and the two decathletes begin to set up the hurdles.

They set them up all along the 110-metre course, pacing off the distance from one barrier to the next. Everything is exact, everything as it would be in competition. There will not be much time between Thompson's return home from California and his going to Götzis. As 1981 was pretty much of a lost year for him, he is being particularly careful now, preparing for every eventuality. Late last autumn he even accepted an invitation to Australia, just so he could gauge the effect of a twenty-six-hour plane trip. Nothing is being left to chance. He is ready to win as he has never been before.

A few nights ago at Briski's, while watching television, one of the three athletes who share the house asked Daley if he had seen the article in December's *Track and Field News* in which Mark Anderson, second place finisher at the National Collegiate Athletic Association decathlon championships with 8171 points, said that he thought it would take 8800 to win the gold medal in Los Angeles, and that, adding up all his best scores, he could be close.

Thompson forced a smile. 'If I'm there, it'll take a little more than that,' he said. 'First of all, doing it on those two days is a little more than adding up your best scores, and second, the score doesn't matter. Oh, if somebody scores 8800, he ought to win it. It could take 7000 and it could take 9000, depending on the conditions. But the score's irrelevant. He'll have to beat me to win.'

That conversation plays over my mind as I watch

Thompson and Zeniou run the hurdles, one starting the other then watching him run, timing him, urging him on, correcting every flaw, every time an arm is not where it is supposed to be, every time the body does not lean forward enough. I think about all the hours in all the years of work, all for just one thing, to win, to win every time. It is the most uncompromising of goals.

The commitment necessary to reach that goal, regardless of conditions or opponents, is an unnatural one. It is total dedication, to the exclusion of all other things. Such an attitude leaves little room for commercial enterprise – Thompson has already severed his connections with two agents because both men have demanded too much time – and makes a normal social life all but impossible. Yet Thompson does not even envisage another way.

The previous Friday night, the night before the meeting between San Diego state and the University of California Los Angeles track teams at Sportsman Track, Slaney went out with some friends after dinner. Thompson said nothing to him about his plans, but it was clear from his expression that he did not approve.

'He's got no business going out,' he said after Slaney had left. 'He wants to throw 200 feet tomorrow. [Slaney holds the SDSU record with a discus throw of 197 feet 1 inch, and has been working hard to break the 200-foot barrier at a university meet.] He's not going to do it like this. It just doesn't work that way. I'll tell you one thing – I wouldn't be going out the night before a competition.' Unbending. Unnatural. But necessary.

The session with the hurdles is going well; it shows on their faces. Though they have trained hard in their time here, this is their first try at hurdling. The work has paid off. It is just about time to quit, but instead of packing up their gear the two men stand on the grass and talk. Things have gone well and both want to go on. Slaney has finished in the discus cage and has gone over to the outdoor weight-training facility at the northwest corner of the field, a sort of screened-in porch covered with green mesh to keep out the sun, so he is happily occupied. They decide to try a few 100s. Thompson immediately brightens up. Part of him, deep in his heart, is still a sprinter.

They leave the hurdles where they are and walk across the infield to the other straightway, the one right in front of the stands. Saturday afternoon, for the meeting with UCLA, they were packed. Now, 2000 empty seats watch the two men. Zeniou is the first to run, with Thompson coaching and timing from the side. 'More arms, more arms,' he shouts as his friend flashes in front of him. 'Pick it up,' he urges, 'pick it up,' and he cheers as the distance is covered in good time. Zeniou asks how he did as he walks back, regaining his wind, and Thompson holds up the watch. Eleven seconds. Zeniou smiles, and grabs the watch, gesturing with mock aggression for Thompson to get into the starting blocks.

Now Zeniou is coach and timer. He brings his hands sharply together in a clap to simulate the firing of the starter's pistol, and Thompson explodes out of the box. He runs in the typical sprinter's style, with tremendous drive, arms pumping, knees lifting only slightly but his legs stretching out behind to power him forward. Zeniou offers no instruction, but cheers him on. When Daley crosses the line the man with the watch just stands there and looks at the numbers, the expression on his face a mixture of pleasure, disbelief and, once again, resignation. Thompson walks over and takes the wristwatch, then nods with satisfaction.

'We've done our work,' he says. 'We've done good work. Let's try it once more.'

It is now after six o'clock, and the day's work is over. Zeniou has gone into the trainer's room in the large building across the alley; Slaney is still in the weight-lifting hut. Thompson sits on the grass, watching the day as it begins to fade.

'Not a bad day,' I offer.

'Not bad at all.'

188

'You're pleased with the times?'

'They weren't bad.'

'What was that last 100 time?'

'Why?'

'I'm curious.'

'You're going to put it in your book.' The statement comes out as an accusation.

'I thought I might.'

'No chance.'

'Why?'

'Because it's mine. Nobody else has to know.'

I smile, but he doesn't.

'I see some things haven't changed since 1979.'

'That'll never change. I don't like people to know how my training's going. Let them find out in competition. Let them find out in Götzis. That's time enough.'

What they would find out in Austria a month later is that Thompson is even better than they thought. Spurred by a flawless first day that includes a personal best in the 400 and a total point production of 4632 – the best first day ever – he will go on to recapture the world record, scoring 8707 points and defeating a game Jürgen Hingsen by 178 points.

But his true mettle will not be tested until later in the summer. At a club meeting on 3 July, after winning the 100 and the hurdles, his pole will shatter in a vault attempt, lacerating his arm and putting him into a cast for three weeks. Then, while he is just getting back into training, his world record will be broken by Hingsen by 16 points at the same kind of all-German decathlon where Kratschmer broke Thompson's record in 1980.

The world would have to wait but three weeks for Thompson's response. The arena: the European Championships in Athens, Greece. There, with the international athletics community looking on, he will put on an awesome show. He will finish the first day with a lead of 114 points over Hingsen. Then, after winning the hurdles on the second day, he will throw badly in his first two attempts with the discus, then calmly propel the wood and steel plate 45.48 metres, a metre farther than in any previous decathlon. After nine events, the competition for the gold will be over, only the question of the world record remaining. But in a stadium where daytime temperatures approach 100, the 1500-metre run will loom as a punishing climax to two days of competition. Going into the final lap, Thompson will appear well out of reach of the record. Then, as the lap begins, Guido Kratschmer will pass him, yelling to him as he does. Not even Thompson will hear the exact words over the roar of 70,000 spectators, but he will understand the essence of his old friend's urging. He will respond with a burst of energy no one could think remains. He and Kratschmer will pass one man, pass two men, pass three men in a show more of courage than stamina. Thompson will cover those final 400 metres in 63.5 seconds, registering 4 minutes 26.5 seconds for the full 1500 metres. That will be good enough for a 226-point victory over Hingsen, a gold medal and a new world record of 8744 points. Nearly as satisfying for Thompson, he will avenge his loss of four years before in Prague, the last decathlon he has ever lost. And at the finish of the 1500, as he stands with hands on hips, looking down at Hingsen and the other runners lying on the ground in exhaustion, will anything else be on his mind?

Twenty-seven days later, at the Commonwealth Games in Brisbane, he will first ruffle the establishment's feathers by declining the invitation to carry the English flag during the three-hour opening ceremony – 'My reason for coming 10,000 miles is to compete; nothing can interfere with that' – then go out and score 8410 to win the decathlon by 406 points.

But on this early evening in San Diego, all that is yet to come. And for at least one man there, none of it will come as a surprise, not his attitude towards his event, certainly not his performance. To Daley Thompson, nothing he has accomplished on the track has been a surprise – nothing he has done, nothing he would do, and not even the relatively short time he has taken to do it.

'I'm always hearing about how quickly I've come along,' he says. 'To say that is to base it on the people that came before me, which is not necessarily the best thing to base it on. I know. I used to make the same mistake.'

I ask what he means, and he pauses for a full minute. We are sitting on the cool grass. He has his arms wrapped around his knees, his legs pulled up toward his chest. 'When I was young,' he begins, 'I thought I could do anything, be anything I wanted, so long as I wanted it badly enough and worked hard. Then I started listening to people who told me about limitations. Over and over I'd hear, "Well, you can't do that – nobody else has ever done it." I couldn't give a damn about what anybody else has done. As far as I'm concerned, they've all got clay feet.

'But when you're young and you hear that stuff, you believe it. Like I'll be shot putting and I'll say I'm going to throw 17 metres. I'll hear, "That's impossible for somebody your size." You don't think about it then, but you remember it, and it works on you.'

I ask who these people are, and he shakes me off. 'It isn't important,' he says. 'The only thing important is that I don't listen any more. But I'm only just now getting over some of the effects. Spending my time with Zeni and Richard, it's easier for me. I think they honestly believe I can do anything. That's good for me. It's better than listening to people who think with limitations.'

Across the field, Richard Slaney has finished his workout and is approaching. From where we sit on the ground, he looks even larger than he is. Thompson slaps at a mosquito on his arm, then gets to his feet. Scattered on the ground are the various shoes he has used in the course of the afternoon's training, shoes for long jump, others for hurdles and for the 100. He starts to put them into his bag and then stops.

'I listened to a lot of that for a long time, but not

now,' he says. 'I'm back to thinking again I can do anything I want to. If I put my mind to it, and as long as it's not outrageous, I can do anything.'

He drops the last pair of shoes into the bag and slings the strap over his shoulder. Then he and Slaney head off to find the Greek. It's late – nearly seven o'clock. Time to get home, have dinner, and watch a little television before bed.

Tomorrow, it starts all over again.

Career Highlights

1976 Montreal Olympic Games: 7435 points – 18th

1977 Götzis International Decathlon: 7921 points – 3rd (world junior record)
Madrid Invitational: 8190 points – 1st

1978 Edmonton Commonwealth Games: 8467 points – 1st (Commonwealth record)

1980 Götzis International Decathlon: 8622 points – 1st (world record)
Moscow Olympics: 8495 points – 1st

1982 Götzis International Decathlon: 8707 points – 1st (world record)
Athens European Championships: 8743 points – 1st (world record)

100 metres	10.51 seconds
Long jump	7.80 metres
Shot put	15.44 metres
High jump	2.03 metres
400 metres	47.11 seconds
First day total	4549 points
110-metre hurdles	14.39 seconds
Discus	45.48 metres
Pole vault	5.00 metres
Javelin	63.56 metres
1500 metres	4:26.5

Brisbane Commonwealth Games: 8410 points – 1st

Index